The Play of the
Platonic Dialogues

Literature and the Sciences of Man

Peter Heller
General Editor

Vol. 12

PETER LANG
New York • Washington, D.C./Baltimore
Bern • Frankfurt am Main • Berlin • Vienna • Paris

Bernard Freydberg

The Play of the Platonic Dialogues

PETER LANG
New York • Washington, D.C./Baltimore
Bern • Frankfurt am Main • Berlin • Vienna • Paris

Library of Congress Cataloging-in-Publication Data

Freydberg, Bernard.
The play of the Platonic dialogues/ Bernard Freydberg.
p. cm. — (Literature and the sciences of man; vol. 12)
Includes bibliographical references and indices.
1. Plato. Dialogues. 2. Play (Philosophy). I. title. II. Series.
B398.P74   184—dc20   96-6888
ISBN 0-8204-3313-6
ISSN 1040-7928

Die Deutsche Bibliothek-CIP-Einheitsaufnahme

Freydberg, Bernard:
The play of the Platonic dialogues/ Bernard Freydberg. –New York;
Washington, D.C./Baltimore; Bern; Frankfurt am Main; Berlin;
Vienna; Paris: Lang.
(Literature and the sciences of man; Vol. 12)
ISBN 0-8204-3313-6
NE: GT

For Akiko

and Malika

ACKNOWLEDGEMENTS

I am grateful once again and always to my colleagues in the Slippery Rock University philosophy department, and to my university. It has been a singular stroke of good fortune to belong to a department in which rigorous discussion and critique is accompanied by philosophical friendship. It is also a blessing to be part of a good university which is far enough from the limelight to allow for and to encourage such work as *Imagination and Depth in Kant's Critique of Pure Reason* (my first book) and *The Play of the Platonic Dialogues*, both of which present more freely developed views and explore them more daringly than is usual in the established scholarship. Like its predecessor, the first draft of this book was written while on a sabbatical leave (fall semester of 1994) granted by my generous colleagues and administrators.

My editor Peter Heller, whose close and critical reading is a valuable gift, contributed in a major way to the improvement of this book. His insightful and incisive work enabled me to strengthen the presentation of what is valuable and original, and to eliminate much that wasn't. I am very grateful to him. Thanks also to Jacques Duvoisin and Richard Findler, who contributed helpful comments on key sections.

The work of John Sallis has inspired my own for some time. While my books and papers stand on their own and often have taken a different path than the one he has followed, I know that I could not have found my own without him.

The Play of the Platonic Dialogues has grown out of a decade-long concern with the role of play in Plato. It stands as an independent work, which presents a sustained and unified interpretation which has been in progress for some time but was not fully formed until late 1993, when I first felt the full force of *Phaedo* 100a3–a8 on truth, and envisioned its relation to play. Prior to this, several journals and societies have given me the opportunity to present my thoughts on Plato as this interpretation was silently taking shape. Some of the material in this book had its genesis in papers I have published or read, but has been so extensively revised as to be unrecognizable in most cases. I wish to thank the journals "Man and World" (Pennsylvania State University) for publishing a Nietzsche paper on myth in which certain ideas on Plato's *Phaedrus* first crystallized, "History of European Ideas" (Pergamon Press) for publishing "*Mythos* and *Logos* in Platonic *Politeiai*" which comprises most of Chapter 6, and K. Boudouris who edited *The Philosophy of Socrates: Ethics, Elenchus and Truth*, which included my paper on Socrates and Aristophanes, a paper which comprises much of Chapter 8. Many thanks also to the Society for the Contemporary Assessment of Platonism (led by Mary Carman Rose, Goucher College), the Society of Ancient Greek Philosophy (led by Anthony Preus, SUNY Binghamton), the International Center for Philosophy and Interdisciplinary Research (led by Leonidas Bargeliotes, University of Athens), the International Society for the Study of European Ideas (led by Ezra Talmor, Haifa University), the International Society for Greek Philosophy (led by K. J. Boudouris, Athens), the Nietzsche Society (in connection with the Society for Phenomenological and Existential Philosophy), the West Virginia Philosophical Association (led by Fred Seddon, Wheeling College), and finally my own regional association, the Tri-State Philosophical Association (led by Ken Lucey, SUC Fredonia).

All of these organizations provided the precious gift of an opportunity for dialogue with colleagues. The broad range of organizations before which I spoke brought me a wide range of comments and criticisms, and this book has surely been strengthened in the process.

On the preparation of the manuscript, I thank Janie McFarland, philosophy department secretary, Kathy Flynn of Bailey Library, and Patti Pink in our data processing office. Further thanks go to students Rod Miller and Holland Williams for their good work toward the preparation of indices and bibliography, and to Malika Hadley Freydberg for help with endnotes. I am very grateful to Diane Bowser, who proofread the manuscript with care and precision.

Special thanks must go to Sharon Furman, who designed and ordered the text with her characteristic expertise and graciousness, and who deserves a paragraph all to herself.

Finally, I offer my abiding gratitude for all things to my wife Akiko Kotani.

NOTE ON TRANSLATION

I have consulted many translations in preparing this book. The occasional changes I have made in them were intended almost always to highlight the literal meanings of key terms. A list of translations consulted appears below. I am very grateful for the fine editions I used, having found the art of translation as fiendishly difficult to practice oneself as it is easy to criticize in others.

My primary text was the Oxford Classical Text, to which page references in my text conform.

The Collected Dialogues of Plato, ed. Hamilton & Cairns (Princeton: Princeton University Press, 1989).

Meno, tr., Grube (Indianapolis: Hackett Publishing Co., 1984).

Plato, vol. I, tr. Fowler (Cambridge: Harvard University Press, The Loeb Classical Library, 1914).

Plato, vol. VII, tr. Bury (Cambridge: Harvard University Press, The Loeb Classical Library, 1952).

The Republic of Plato, tr. Bloom, Allan (New York: Basic Books, 1968).

The Symposium and the Phaedrus: Plato's Erotic Dialogues, tr. Cobb (Albany: SUNY Press, 1993).

TABLE OF CONTENTS

Part III: Play and the Soul

FOREWORD

"... .we must go through our lives playing (*paizonta*) at certain pastimes (*paidias*). . ."[1]

Laws (803e1)

This study will expose the playfulness at the heart of the Platonic dialogues. But just as the dialogues disclose a philosophical rigor at their heart, *The Play of the Platonic Dialogues* will present a rigorous interpretation of them, especially those in which play is explicitly featured or occurs most prominently. In Plato as in no other thinker, play and seriousness are intertwined, and this interpretation will attempt to do justice to the dialogues by tracing the weaves of this intertwining and by interpreting its philosophical content both in its context and in its general significance. While there are many fine books on Plato, none thematizes play so prominently and develops its role in so thorough a fashion.[2]

Two large concerns drive this study. The first and more general one is the desire to get the Platonic dialogues right. This desire can be satisfied only through faithfulness both to their way of philosophizing and to their subject matter. The strictures of the interpretation are set by the dialogues. It will respect the limits set by them and the terms found in them. The other major concern is the kinship of philosophy and play. *The Play of the Platonic*

Dialogues aims to show that any truly accurate appraisal of the Platonic dialogues requires the recognition of play as fundamentally constitutive of them.

The first chapter, entitled "Play in Plato," sets out the general view clearly and contrasts it with certain competitors. Playfulness in Plato is never frivolous or merely decorative, but always has philosophical content. Playfulness is aligned with measure; seriousness loosed from play also loses its genuine philosophical bearing. Anchoring philosophy and Platonic thought in play—this is what sets my book apart. I will show how the "large" issues in Plato (the theory of forms, of the state, of recollection, of the immortality of the soul and the rest) are functions of play before they are anything else.

There is, in other words, a healthy and philosophically central strain which runs through Plato (and in subtle ways through the tradition to the present) which has little to do with reason or rationalism and nearly as little to do with the generation of the traditional philosophical and scientific disciplines such as metaphysics, physics, ethics, psychology and logic. I became aware of this strain first through the work of John Sallis, whose *Being and Logos: The Way of the Platonic Dialogues*[3] grants fundamental status to play more than any other. Despite the apparent radicalness of many of his views, his interpretations are rooted directly in the Platonic texts. While Sallis' interpretation moves away from seeing the dialogues primarily as documents for the history and virtue of rational argumentation and toward philosophy as ongoing thoughtful wonder,[4] the line of interpretation he discloses is rigorous and measured. Before moving on to my own way of developing this strain, here are the features of Sallis' approach I find particularly distinctive and valuable:

1) More clearly than any other Plato interpreter for whom the drama of the dialogues carries great weight, Sallis notes the equal status of *mythos* among the basic elements of the dialogue. "Whatever the final character of the contrast [between *mythos* and *logos*] may be, what is of utmost importance initially is that *mythos* not be taken, in advance, as an inferior kind of *logos*, as a meager substitute for something else intrinsically more desirable, as a mere compromise between knowledge and the *logos*

appropriate to it, on the one hand, and sheer ignorance and its inevitable silence, on the other hand."[5] And his book ends with the citation of a *mythos* within a *mythos*, the final words from the myth of Er in the *Republic*.

Sallis allows the mythical dimension of the dialogue to speak as a full voice, rather than merely to echo or to illustrate. *Mythos* in Sallis becomes an originary way of showing, with which and against which the other dialogical elements work and play. The importance of recognizing *mythos* as no less fundamental than *logos* for both a proper scholarly reading of Plato and for gaining access to the playfulness of the dialogues cannot be overemphasized. The dialogues can now speak in their own terms, without some pre-emptive interpretation relegating the mythical part to a secondary status inconsistent with the texts of the dialogues themselves.

2) For Sallis, *logos* is not something settled by the Platonic dialogues, or employed by them in order to present or refute philosophical views. It does not only mean "rational argument," however well some *logoi* conform to this definition. As Sallis notes by combing the most accessible surface of the dialogues, we find *logoi* of criticism (Book I, *Republic*), eristic (*Euthydēmus*), mathematics (*Meno*), beyond mathematics (*Republic* VI-VII), imagery (sun analogy), and about *logos* (*Cratylus*—etymology).[6]

Logos, which we will here preliminarily and loosely understand as speech and language bound up with thought,[7] occurs for us in many guises. These various ways of *logos* are made manifest and brought to awareness nowhere more than near the beginning of the history of philosophy, in the Platonic dialogues.

There is surely something to be gained by isolating those arguments which are in some way interesting from the point of view of contemporary problems in ethics, political philosophy, epistemology, et al., and/or by disclosing or reconstructing them in a logically rigorous manner. But this is just one aspect of the dialogues, and is at play with all of the others. By contrast, I will seek to situate *logoi* on such topics as the intelligibility of virtue, the philosopher-king, and the forms within this play and as part of it.

3) On *play*, Sallis' interpretation is at its most tantalizing. No interpreter so unmistakably isolates and celebrates the role of play in the dialogues,

although many have noted its presence. His is the insight—provocatively breached in his book but deserving of further development—that I now take up and follow out in this book.

In a dense two pages,[8] Sallis declares play to be nothing less than the appropriate entrance to philosophy, and its appropriate practice. He notes that play takes many forms in the dialogues, but that it is most apparent in those dialogues which, like the *Cratylus*, take the form of comedy. Play must be lawful, must be bound to something beyond itself. But as playthings of the gods, we are already given over to the very playfulness that we enact when we philosophize. As usual, all of Sallis' insights are clearly traceable to passages in the Platonic texts. They are gathered in order to let the playfulness of the dialogues shine forth *from* the dialogues.

My first chapter will develop and expand upon these insights in order to prepare the way for the expositions to follow. The interpretation guiding them issues from that healthy, vigorous strain which can now be characterized further with components drawn from the dialogues: a darkness-acknowledging *mythos*, a self-questioning *logos*, related to one another in a measure-giving *play* which acknowledges a certain distance from wisdom but maintains a cheerfulness in the midst of this distance.[9] There are many places in the dialogues from which one could locate a point of departure for this fateful strain. I choose the *Apology* because its familiarity is equal to its appropriateness for the purpose.

The generation of Socrates' "wisdom" is well known. Having examined politicians, poets and artisans and finding them wanting in wisdom, he declares his own ignorance to be at least no worse—and his recognition of it perhaps more worthy—than their unawareness of theirs. In the course of this examination, the famous Socratic *elenchos* (refutation by cross-examination; its plural is *elenchoi*) is displayed in its philosophical splendor. It justifies no knowledge claim, but debunks much pretentiousness. Its use in other dialogues discloses the confusion dwelling at the heart of the thoughts of many of Socrates' interlocutors, and occasionally discloses confusion in Socrates as well.

Interpretations of the *elenchos* abound. A worthy one from the Anglo-

American tradition is offered by Donald Davidson, who divorces the issue of the *elenchos* from the pursuit of truth and concludes that its principal role is to further the end of clarifying our basic concepts through human conversation, an end which is Socrates' as well: "Dialogue, particularly in the form of the *elenchos*, provides the forum in which alone words take on meaning and concepts are slowly clarified."[10] Thus, *elenchos* is a rational process whereby all-too-human confusion is rendered less confused, perhaps becoming gradually clearer.

This is hardly the last word on Socrates' way of cross-examination, merely the sparsest. Socratic practice has an equally influential mythical source, which Davidson either denies or ignores. He claims not to take seriously Socrates' recourse to his *daimonion*, and takes no note whatsoever of the saying of the god. Instead, he makes the groundless conjecture that Socrates would have listened to such sources "only if he thought them rational."[11]

But the dialogue clearly indicates that Socratic wisdom has a non-rational source! Word of the god at Delphi which declares no one wiser than Socrates, and which was spoken through a priestess to friend and democrat Chaerophon, is offered as evidence for this wisdom. I maintain that the *elenchos* and its result cannot be properly understood apart from such mythical sources. At first, Socrates expresses puzzlement at the oracle, for he claims no wisdom. Then, he tries to refute the god by means of a standard elenctic move: he tries to find one wiser person. Only upon his failure in this quest does he suppose that the god might be referring to the paltriness of human wisdom, and the merit of acknowledging this paltriness like Socrates did. That is to say, the questioning of the citizens of Athens is bound up with the questioning of the god. But how can one question a god?

For reasons which will become clear in chapter 8, the *Apology* appears to be one of the least mythical and least playful of the dialogues. Yet, this healthy strain can be seen even here. The bond of Socrates to the non-rational source is unquestioned, even though this source is mediated at least twice, by the priestess and by Chaerophon. In other words, the dialogue presents a distance between the philosopher and the non-rational source, a distance both from divinity and from the doubly mediated oracle. This very distance allows for the play of Socrates and the god on the "playground" of Athens. Thus, we have the simultaneously mirroring play of Socrates (1) testing the riddle of the god by trying to find someone wiser, and in so doing stirring up the citizens of Athens who he now seeks to educate in the god's name and (2) testing/educating the Athenians in terms of their pretensions to wisdom, which discloses that Socrates is the one than whom no one is wiser, as the god said. (21a4–6)

What ultimately makes Athens a playground in the *Apology* is the defanging of death as a danger to a good human being. No human being of worth, we are told, takes it into account when deciding to act. (28d6–29b9) In this very profound sense, the apparent *hubris* of Socrates' testing of the god together with the apparent danger of angering the citizens of Athens occur as *play*. The defense of Socrates unfolds as a drama of the highest seriousness, but one in which no harm is either done or suffered by anyone (". . .to a good man no harm (*kakon*) can come in life or after." [41d1–2])

On this reading, the *elenchos* retains its full power and significance as philosophical instrument, and in a certain sense can be excerpted from the dialogical context and located as an important moment in the history of Western philosophy. This has been done by Gregory Vlastos, the interpreter best known for separating Plato from Socrates in the dialogues and for inspiring exploration of the implications of this separation. In this division of men and of philosophical orientations, Plato is looked upon as a bungler whose unfortunate metaphysical commitments did little honor to his teacher while Socrates is seen as a truly significant contributor to rational philosophical criticism.

The mystery is not that such an interpretation has arisen and found influence, for it provides the Anglo-American approach to philosophy with historical rooting, however difficult it may be to imagine Socrates as a precursor of articles for *Journal of Philosophy* on physicalism and extensionalism. But it is hard to fathom how such an interpretation is not seen as being driven by extra-textual needs and by assumptions that the dialogues themselves call into question, often quite forcefully. One such assumption is the minor significance (if not utter insignificance) ascribed to myth and play, in the face of the clearly large place they occupy in the Platonic texts. Another is the belief that Plato was trying to form philosophical theories along the lines of those formed in the academic specialties within contemporary analytic philosophy departments. Without addressing the value or lack of value of such assumptions, there is little if any actual textual support in Plato for either one.

It may be helpful for the location of *The Play of the Platonic Dialogues* on the map of Plato interpretation to set forth a few beliefs about Platonic philosophy which are both widespread and more particular than the two assumptions mentioned in the previous paragraph. Readers who wish may keep them in mind throughout, and I will return to them briefly and serially in the conclusion. But as I believe that the Platonic philosophy is eviscerated when treated as a set of responses to certain issues considered in abstraction from their place in the dialogues, they will be treated extensively in their context rather than separately.

Here are four particularly prominent assumptions:

1) The dialogues try to replace mythical explanations with rational ones.

2) The forms (*eidē*) are ideal objects of some kind, perhaps belonging to another world.

3) Virtue is knowledge.

4) The dialogues advocate some form of censorship of the arts.

When the playfulness of the dialogues is enacted by the reader, or when the interpreter becomes "though in a different way—one of the interlocutors of the dialogue,"[12] these issues are exposed as the second-order red herrings that they are, and philosophy in the genuine spirit of the dialogues can begin again.

PART I

PLAY AND THE ACTIVITY
OF PHILOSOPHY

CHAPTER ONE:
PLAY IN PLATO

Alfred North Whitehead's ambiguous celebration of Plato gives us excellent entry into Plato's thought on play, for it opens out several key lines of exploration. In *Adventures of Ideas*, he makes the proclamation that "Plato divined the seven main factors interwoven in fact:—The Ideas, The Physical Elements, The Psyche, The Eros, The Harmony, The Mathematical Relations, The Receptacle. All philosophical systems are endeavors to express the interweaving of these components."[13] But this celebration of Plato as the eternal task-setter for future toilers is quickly set off by a picture of Plato as a primitive bungler: "Of course, it is most unscholarly to identify our modern notions with these archaic thoughts of Plato. For us everything has a subtle difference."[14] Plato was a diviner, whose ultimate recourse was to intuition, while we are reasoners seeking better and better generalizations.

Of course, both elements of intellect and elements of inspiration are present in the Platonic dialogues. They serve both as silent actuators of the dialogues and as subjects treated by the dialogues. For example, the search for truth by means of the intellect gives rise to philosophical issues treated in the dialogues, and intellect itself is a subject treated in the dialogues, e.g. in the discussion of the divided line in Book VI of the *Republic*. Similarly, inspiration generates images of philosophical significance in the dialogues, and inspiration itself is a subject treated, e.g. in the *Ion*. Play, the subject of this chapter, is not numbered among Whitehead's seven major factors which purportedly make up the weave of our heritage. Nor is play identifiable with either of the two subjects/actuators mentioned above, or with some combination of them. Rather, play is the most fundamental way the elements of the Platonic dialogues both relate to one another and to components within each one considered separately. Like intellect and inspiration, play is both an actuating impulse which gives rise to matters discussed in the dialogues, and a subject treated in many of them.

In one sense, this book is intended as a contribution to Plato scholarship which advances the understanding of the fundamental philosophical significance of what has all-too-carelessly been called the "dramatic" or "literary" side of the dialogues, as if one or the other "side" could be sectioned off without serious consequence to the integrity of the whole. But it is also intended to note and to advance an idea of play which has crept into our general philosophical discourse, often without notice, more and more in contemporary philosophy. The confidence of the analytic side of our tradition to solve all or nearly all "genuine" philosophical problems has crumbled. The continental side no longer seeks the all-embracing phenomenological system or account of being. Since the thoroughgoing rigor of philosophy once hoped for is now regarded as something between a beautiful dream and a conceit, the notion of play seems well suited for elevation to respectability if not centrality. From the continental side, I offer a passage from Derrida which notes this loss of hope for large-scale interpretive success and its implication for philosophy. It can serve as both specimen and emblem:

> There are thus two interpretations of interpretation, of structure, of sign, of freeplay. The one seeks to decipher, dreams of deciphering, a truth or an origin which is free from freeplay or from the order of the sign and lives like an exile the necessity of interpretation. The other, which is no longer turned toward the origin affirms freeplay and tries to pass beyond man and humanism, the name of man being the name of that being who, throughout the history of metaphysics or

of ontotheology—in other words through the history of all history—has dreamed of full presence, the reassuring foundation, the origin and the end of the game.[15]

Here, play (freeplay) functions as an approach to interpretation without the imposition of the tradition which has governed and perhaps calcified the activity of interpretation by referring it to an origin as a giver of meaning. Play provides escape and refuge from traditional constraints.

The phenomenon of play (if not the word) has also made its entrance on what might be called the lapsed-analytic side of contemporary philosophy, in the work of Richard Rorty. In *Philosophy and the Mirror of Nature*, Rorty brings together systematic strains (problem-oriented, traditional-epistemological, primarily Anglo-American style philosophy) and edifying strains of philosophy (which are neither mainstream nor problem-oriented but are influential and challenging, such as those issuing from the work of Wittgenstein, Dewey and Heidegger) by declaring their juncture in the conversation of the West. This conversation is neither the progressive unfolding of philosophical truth through the solving of problems nor the recasting of philosophy along new lines of edification: "The conversational interest of philosophy as a subject, or some individual philosopher of genius, has varied and will continue to vary in unpredictable ways depending upon contingencies."[16] One can justly characterize such a conversation as playful since it allows and displays movement unconstrained by any implicit or explicit agenda. After indicating that "we can continue the conversation Plato began without discussing the topics Plato discussed," he writes that "the conversation Plato began has been enlarged by more voices than Plato would have dreamed possible, and thus (!) by topics he knew nothing of."[17] (emphasis mine) Thus we may characterize Rorty's post-Platonic play as allowing for an unrestricted ongoing edifying/critical conversation. Like Derrida, Rorty disdains any recourse to an origin which governs the conversation. It seems fair to link the two as advocates of a playful openness toward previously closed off possibilities.

We can even detect a glimmer of play in the statements of such hard advocates of philosophy in a scientific cast as Quine, who has said,

"Inspirational and edifying writing is admirable, but the place for it is the novel, the poem, the sermon, or the literary essay. Philosophers in the professional sense have no peculiar fitness for it."[18] While he grants nothing like play within the discipline proper as he understands it, he notes that the separation of philosophers into cranks and sages has not followed the analogous separations among scientists and among "the minor domestic ruminants into sheep and goats." But, he finds this "perhaps as it should be, in view of the unregimented and speculative nature of the subject," in other words because there is play at least at the entrance to philosophy.[19]

But what does this play consist of? How can we characterize it? Thus far, it seems to be nothing more than a certain indeterminism. Its origin and even its description are negative. Play is interpretation *not* governed by an origin, *not* delimited by a preadopted set of meanings or system of meaning. Or play is the conversation *not* governed by any particular set of problems and/or foundational assumptions. Or else play enters when *lack* of regulation allows it, e.g. into speculative enterprises. If play is not itself negative, the most that can be said in light of the previous formulations is that when other, more serious pursuits or attitudes break down, one has recourse to play. Governing the entrance of play, then, is a kind of absence. Play itself may be the marker of this absence.

In the case of the idea of play, we are called to philosophy's past in Plato not merely for historical information on its origin but also for a certain guidance. In Plato, play occurs not merely as an expedient when more serious efforts have failed but as foundational to philosophic activity, as intrinsic to the Platonic way of philosophizing and as serious itself, perhaps more so than the seriousness of the philosophical styles and doctrines spoken of above. A look at Plato's treatment of play may well serve to inform today's philosophical plight substantively, and by this means serve to show that just as Plato remains in our past as our basis, so he also remains in our future.

Sallis has observed of philosophy in Plato that "whatever else may pertain to it and its beginning, philosophy is begun in play. It is in play that one begins to philosophize and, at least to the extent that it is this beginning that the dialogues aim to provoke, their playfulness is appropriate and calls for a responsive play on the part of the one who seeks to interpret them."[20] Nor does this playfulness cease with philosophical maturity or even adolescence. In Plato's *Phaedrus*, a written work and a philosophical work, we read that

> the one who thinks that in the written word there is necessarily much that is playful, and that no written discourse, whether in meter or in prose, is worthy of being treated with great seriousness. . . but that the best of [written works] really serve to remind us of what we know. . .is likely to be such as you and I might pray that we ourselves may become. (277e5-278b4)

Such a wise man also thinks that only the forms ". . .spoken and really written in a soul in clearness and perfection have serious value." (278a2–5) If we interpret this passage directly and seriously, it seems to offer the doctrine that only what is truly and deeply and correctly conceived in the soul matters in any substantive way, and that all external writing falls short of this ideal conception. But if Sallis' suggestion of responsive play is heeded in the interpretation, the outcome is different.

First of all, the words of the dialogue (which are written) are directing the reader to interpret them playfully, and along with this the reader is warned not to interpret them "with great seriousness." Thus, the words are to be taken playfully and with *some* seriousness. What might be serious in this passage? Perhaps the claim that the truly wise man Socrates and Phaedrus (since they are philosophers) would pray to become has the forms (*eidē*) inscribed in his soul clearly and perfectly and pays attention to nothing else than them and to teaching them to others. For the sake of argument, this claim will be regarded as the position of Socrates. The playful side of this position is that there is no such being on earth. Surely neither Socrates nor Phaedrus regard their souls as having such clear and perfect inscriptions in them. Therefore, the notion that a seriousness which transcends all playfulness is an actual human possibility is playfully closed off.

The other serious proclamation is the one which says that the best of written discourses serve only to remind us of what we know (*eidotōn hupomnēsin*). (278a1) Now in a straightforward, "serious" sense, this says that the best written works enable us to recollect the forms (*eidē*) in the manner discussed in the *Meno* and in the *Phaedrus*. According to such a straightforward interpretation, we may not be able to achieve the perfect knowledge of the truly wise man, but we might approach this knowledge to the degree that our abilities allow. Again, this view will be regarded as Socrates' for the sake of the argument. But reading this passage playfully, the recollection of what we know becomes just as much a recollection of the ignorance to which we are given over. Thus, we recollect our distance from this perfect knowledge, and with this distance we remind ourselves that we are closed off from anything of great seriousness.

In these reflections, we begin to see the inversion suggested earlier. Unlike our contemporary situation in which play emerges out of a breakdown in a certain kind of philosophical seriousness, here in Plato a certain kind of philosophical seriousness occurs as a transgression of the limits established in the founding play. In *Republic* IV, "lawful play" initiates education "straightaway." Law-abiding, good men are formed "when the boys make a fine (*kalos*) beginning at play and receive lawfulness (*eunomian*) from music. . . ."(425a3-a4) Still further, play is the initiation into the more serious lawfulness they will later enter upon as citizens:

> . . . Mustn't our boys take part in more lawful play straightaway, since, if play becomes lawless itself and the children along with it, it's not possible that they'll grow up to be law-abiding, good men. . . (424e5-425a1)

It may appear from these passages that play for Plato is a generic concept with "lawful" and "lawless" as its two species, and in a certain sense such an extraction of this view is accurate. But the dialogue's unfolding suggests that play most truly manifests itself not in terms of lawful- and lawlessness, but in relation to a more basic phenomenon.

The passage in which Socrates argues for the restriction from partaking in arguments at too young an age seems to be a clear case for the view of play as a merely generic concept:

An older man, however . . . will imitate and consider the truth rather than the one who plays and contradicts for the sake of the game. (539c5-c9)

And Sallis argues that this "reference is to a kind of play which, in contrast to that exemplified in the philosophical exchange between Socrates and Glaucon, is not lawful, not bound by anything beyond itself."[21] This passage is likened to the one in the *Laws* which concerns "harmless pleasure" which has grace (*charitos*) as its only concomitant. It reads: ". . . I call this [pleasure (*hēdonēn*) which aims at grace alone] also play (*paidian*), whenever the harm or help it does is not worth bringing seriously to *logos*." (667e2–8) Here, play is given simply as gracefulness for its own sake, and as antecedent to the more philosophically serious determinations of play-in-service-to-lawfulness or play-in-service-to-truth. In both dialogues the initiating play is characterized not by law or its absence, but by the gracefulness belonging to music which is akin to it by nature.

Even the lawlessness spoken of at *Republic* 424d2 is not absence of law. *Paranomia* indicates something closer to transgression of law or order, and *paranomos* accordingly means action contrary to law. The clear implication is that even the most minimal notion of harmless pleasure-giving music includes a notion of lawful order as the correlate of that pleasure. Thus, this pleasure is called play on account of its separation from the serious matters of truth/falsity, goodness/badness and, in a political sense, lawfulness/ unlawfulness. But it can be called play at all only because of its appropriation to the measure of grace (*charitos*), to an order in which the human things must participate in some way in order to be things of play. In more modern terms, lawful play is the condition for the possibility of lawless play.

In this light, the younger man "who plays and contradicts for the sake of the game" of arguments is not contrasted with the serious older man, but with the one whose play is given over to what appropriately governs it, i.e. the strictures of music and gymnastic, which are properly introduced long before the contradicting art of dialectic within the subject of *logoi*. Premature dialectic engenders deformity of play. That is, insufficient exposure of the soul to the playful ordering of music and of the body deprives the human being of the appropriate preparation for receiving *logoi*. The sense of measure instilled through music and exercise enables the soul to receive *logoi* with proper measure. Such deprivation begets deformed treatment of argument. Without the gracefulness of music to inform it, one's play is bound to nothing beyond itself, to use Sallis' formulation. But play bound to nothing beyond itself is nothing other than play unbound from the conditions which first made it possible. With respect to *logos*, this playing and contradicting for the sake of the game can be seen as play unbound from the order of truth, an order which the order of grace (*charitos*) precedes as initiator for the youth.[22] The entire discussion, in fact, is governed by the view expressed that play (and not force) must be the foundation of the education of the free human being, and that this playful education, even in arguments, must be enacted by those with "orderly and stable natures" (539d4) in whom lawfulness has been instilled by the measured play of graceful music. The deforming flatterers introduce transgression (*paranomia*) of the orderly, stable realm of lawfulness (*nomos*).

Play's relation to seriousness may be treated in a similar fashion. Seriousness is not the opposite of play any more than lawfulness is. Let us consider several passages from the *Republic*:

Mustn't we first come to an agreement whether these things [e. g. men and women exercising naked together] are possible or not, and give anyone who wants to dispute—whether it's a man who likes to play or one who is serious—the opportunity to dispute. . . (452e4-e7)

'I forgot,' I said 'that we were playing and . . . spoke rather intensely. For as I was talking I looked at philosophy and, seeing her undeservedly spattered with mud, I seem to have been vexed and said what I had to say too spiritedly . . .' (536c1-c5)

. . . Imitation is a kind of play and not serious; and those who take up tragic poetry in iambic and epics are all imitators in the highest degree. (602b8-b10)

The first and third passages clearly refer play to music, a recurring theme in the *Republic*. Thus far, its initiatory role as the correlate of childlike play within the order of grace (*charitos*) has been stressed. In these passages, play is ascribed to more specific musical regions: the comedies of Aristophanes (especially *Ecclesiazousai*—the title is sometimes given in English as *The Assembly of Women*) and perhaps others (the "men who like to play" in the first passage, who were begged "not to mind their own business, but to be serious" at 452c5-6[23]), and the works of the classical tragedians in the third. It is not the purpose at this early stage to address the perennial issue in Plato of the proper approach to Greek music (epic, comedy, tragedy). Even without such a discussion, it is clear that the playfulness of the musical/poetical works always occurs in concert with seriousness and measure. Socrates' comedian of and for the first passage does the measured work of playfully ridiculing what is ridiculous (thereby disclosing the truly serious side). And the tragic and epic poets' play is likewise given over to the most serious issues for human beings. Both are governed by melodic and metrical structures which introduce a measure of order and stability within their inspiration.

Thus, the seriousness to which play is contrasted in these passages is, perhaps ironically, an inappropriate seriousness. It is seriousness divorced from play which, in its most genuine Platonic sense, occurs as measure-giving play. The second quotation indicates that this is the best reading of the relation of play and seriousness, for it signals that play is necessary for speaking appropriately about philosophy and within philosophy. Seriousness occurs under the sway of strong emotion, and this seriousness is inappropriate to the enterprise (as is the engendering excess of spirit). *The Play of the Platonic Dialogues* is a title which does not merely indicate an isolated quality of the dialogues, but also characterizes their basic philosophical orientation.

The comedies, tragedies and epics which are said to be playful without being serious do not lack serious themes. They merely lack a reasoned account of what they present (if indeed such an account properly belongs in them). Only when they are taken as attempting to give a philosophical account do we find these works lacking in seriousness. When they are taken as works of inspiration disclosing important truths to their audiences through a non-rational order (as the *Ion* presents them at 533e3–535a2[24]), they are valuable. In other words, when they are taken seriously, they are playful and not serious. But when we take them playfully, i.e. when we enter these works as initiates into music, they can be both playful and serious. Thus, no sensible man would imitate someone worse "unless it's done in play." (396e2) Only as play are the imitative works suitable for the "properly measured (*metrios*) human being." (396c5)

The *Laws*, while repeating some of the main insights on play of the *Republic*, goes beyond it in its clear proclamation of play not merely as initiator in education, but also as the ultimate purpose of life.[25] As in the *Republic*, it is only by means of play that a human being can properly be initiated into any art and can master one:

> . . . the carpenter should be taught by his play to use the rule and to measure, and the soldier taught horsemanship, and the like. . . First and foremost, education, we say, consists in that right nurture which most strongly draws the soul of the child when at play to a love of that pursuit of which, when he becomes a man, he must possess a perfect mastery. (643c4-d4)

Further, only in play does one reach maximum fulfillment. A man or a woman "playing at the noblest (*kallistas*) pastimes" (803c7) enacts the best life. After extolling peace over war, the Athenian stranger asks and answers a crucial question:

> What, then, is the right way? We should live out our lives playing at certain pastimes—sacrificing, singing and dancing—so as to be able to win heaven's favor and to repel our foes and vanquish them in fight. (803d9-e4)

What shall one make of such an answer, which seems to exclude much of value to the good life—not least, philosophy? First, all three activities involve the introduction of measure, involve giving oneself over to a certain kind of rule. In sacrificing, one clearly admits one's non-divinity; the offering of something of value to the gods acknowledges that one does not have one's measure entirely within oneself. As to singing and dancing, both are arts which require measure and rule of both body and soul. For Plato, play is associated with rule and measure: this is why it is both fundamental and final. Recall that the supposedly serious and rational Socrates practices music on his final day, writing (among other things) a hymn to Apollo in verse. Death is nothing serious, or rather death receives its proper seriousness when it is confronted playfully.[26] And the Stranger's playful passage from the *Laws* recollects the lawful play at the heart of all things: relation to the gods, music, gymnastic, even warfare. From initiation through death, humankind dwells playfully.

Even the most serious of Platonic "doctrines," the "theory of forms" which orders all knowledge, must be understood as an extension of that initiating play which founds all philosophic discourse. (There is also much play within the so-called theory of forms, which will be taken up in Part I.) Many of the conundrums associated with the theory of forms issue from taking this theory with a seriousness which excludes that play out of which it was born.[27] The play which gives rise to the so-called Platonic "doctrines" is always incorporated within them as well as being incorporated into the way of their presentation.

Bringing all of this to bear upon the concerns expressed earlier, this preliminary analysis of Platonic play begets a peculiar reversal of Whitehead's celebration of Plato (and also of the related reflections of Derrida, Rorty and Quine, in differing degrees). The playful side of thought in the work of those thinkers was allowed entrance as an inverse function of the success of the serious side. Philosophy in the Platonic dialogues is, according to this analysis, fundamentally playful. Seriousness which transgresses the order of philosophical play is to be feared (although the seriousness of philosophical argument is certainly part of the play). Philosophy in Plato always occurs as playful initiation into and encounter with human *logos* as it seeks what is best.

The theories and doctrines engendered belong intimately to its purpose, but are one and all marked by their origin in play. Thus Whitehead is correct (so is Rorty, but in a different and, I think, less significant way) when he says that certain modern notions have surpassed the Platonic ones in subtlety, and (we can add) also predictive power. He is correct, also, when he traces the modern concepts back to their origin in Plato and sees all efforts since as working out their details. But his denigration of what he calls "intuition" and "divining" is surely questionable. Our century has (once again) shown the limits of intellect, the apparently insurmountable difficulty of solving all (or any) philosophical problems, even in principle; thus some version of play is admitted. But a profound sense of play has been shown to dwell already at the heart of the Platonic dialogues. In this light, one must wonder whether the gain in subtlety we enjoy in our science has begotten a corresponding gain (or any) for philosophy.

What does this sense of play have to do with the "divining" and "intuiting" Whitehead regarded with a mixture of praise and disparagement? The Platonic dialogues present not merely a kind of inquiry undertaken long ago, but a way of philosophizing which is ever contemporary. Every attempt at philosophic discourse, however rigorous or formal it may seem, contains elements of "intuition" and "divining." Otherwise there would be no wondering at all, no reason to search, nothing to search with or for. When we philosophize, when we think at all, we are at play. Whatever subsequent efforts to verify or to enlarge or to alter an initiating thought (and whatever the origin and nature of the elements comprising that thought), the playfulness at its source remains directive in some way. The Platonic dialogues recollect this: even in their most laborious and densest efforts, such as the distinction of the philosopher and the sophist (*Sophist*) and the discussion of the receptacle (*Timaeus*), there is an initial and final openness within which the philosophizing proceeds.

The difference today lies not so much in the playfulness of our activity (though there is a large difference in self-conception) but in the way we conceive the purpose of our work. For us, it tends to be taken seriously as an epistemological, moral, aesthetic or existential enterprise, or perhaps even a political one. In Plato the end is play itself.

CHAPTER TWO:
PLAY AND DARKNESS:
MYTH AND METHODOLOGY

Myths in Plato are not didactic instruments which are employed to aid the less gifted in reaching a conclusion that someone brighter could reach by directly rational means. Nor are they mere illustrations of rational ideas or arguments. Myths are likely accounts, tales of matters which cannot otherwise show themselves. The presence of myth indicates "a bond to an element of darkness, in contrast to that which is taken up in the light of *logos*."[28] While both darkness and light belong to all human discourse, *mythos* makes this darkness most prominently manifest through the presence of vivid imagery together with the absence of reasoned accounts and knowledge claims. By contrast, reasons and conclusions rather than inspired images allow *logoi* to bring their matter to light.

The division between myths and reasoned accounts (especially arguments) cannot be indicated by a line between them (for where could one stand so that one could draw such a line?). Their tasks cut across one another. Myths bring to light: the great account of the universe in the *Timaeus*, for example, is told as "a likely myth." (29d1—*ton eikota muthon*) Arguments deliver into darkness: in the *Laches*, for example, neither of two brave generals can begin to say what courage is at the end of a protracted rational inquiry into it. (199e11–12)

Mythos both constitutes and shapes the phenomenon of play decisively in Plato. Some myths appear to be explanatory, like the myth of recollection in the *Meno* or of Prometheus and Epimetheus in the *Gorgias*. Some seem to have founding significance, like the myth of the metals in the *Republic* or of the demiurge in the *Timaeus*. Some, like the account of the true earth in the *Phaedo* or of the spindle of Necessity in the *Republic*, appear to be reports of true but unseen places. But the myths are reducible neither to the issues with which they are connected nor to the conscious purposes of their conveyor. However and wherever they occur, they offer neither conclusions nor rational support for what they say. Rather, myths make a certain experience available: the soul can traverse their vicarious imagery and so can undergo another kind of journey which contributes to the love of wisdom in ways not available through argument.

This imaginative journey which myths invite clearly belongs to the play of the dialogues. Certain beliefs brook no dispute and must be accepted in order to enter their philosophical realm. These can be called serious in a straightforward sense. But myths are not believed (or disbelieved) in this direct way. The participation in these myths, or the interpretation of them, is a matter of the free act of the soul. The soul can take them up from differing perspectives, yielding varying outcomes (as we will see quite dramatically in Chapter 7 with the "Achilles in Hades" myth). By contrast, the dialogues' serious beliefs admit no plausible alternatives regarding their truth, or regarding the conviction that their opposites would make nonsense of the dialogues. Among such serious beliefs are the following: it is better to admit ignorance than to profess knowledge that one lacks; it is better to inquire than to remain content with unexamined ignorance; it is mistaken to fear death; there is nothing more important than the care of one's soul; the political arena has its just claims which must be discharged. All of these inscribe themselves into their readers in a firm fashion. Their subject matter cannot be thought or turned otherwise without tearing the dialogue from its moorings.

But these moorings themselves, as we have already seen, have a mythical element. Myths surround even these serious features in the dialogues. But the myths do not compel, and never proclaim. Rather, the myths elicit. Through images which evoke a wondering response in the soul, myths make their subject matter available for reflection. This reflection can take the form of philosophical questioning, such as the way the Delphic oracle in the *Apology* served to provoke the question of the nature of human wisdom. This reflection can also take the form of a deepening of insight into a matter which is present but difficult to grasp, as love (*Erōs*) is better (though not completely) understood through the myth told in the *Symposium* of its parents *Poros* (Resource) and *Penia* (Poverty) at the divine banquet.[29] Or the reflection can take the form of focusing upon human reflection itself, as in the cave. In all of these cases, the myth calls the soul forth and directs it toward a certain region, allowing the soul its full freedom in its approach to it. The myths *play*. They playfully draw the unhardened soul into the realm of philosophical activity.

By "unhardened," I mean free (or freed) from firm conviction, able to receive material from many sources while holding it at a distance, trusting one's capacity to regard it appropriately. Socrates says he'd be less strange if he were distrustful (*Phaedrus* 229c6—*apistoiēn*) of myths, but this hardly means that he believes them literally. Trust or belief (*pistis*), in this sense, resides as much in the soul's relation to itself and its capacity to seek honestly as it does in relation to certain positions or opinions or images.

This attitude, clearly manifest in relation to myths, is also present in relation to all elements of the dialogues. It can be characterized quite simply as the willingness to take something up respectfully and inquire as to its meaning and significance, whatever its source.[30] It is not only the stance when faced with the charm of myths, but is the posture toward virtually all of the (normally considered) philosophical issues in the dialogues, e.g. the theory of forms, metaphysical and moral intellectualism, the immortality of the soul, and above all the ultimate worthiness of the *logoi* regarding each of these.[31] As I will show, these matters receive a certain emphasis in the dialogues for good philosophical reasons, but are hardly doctrines or theories at all. The only firm beliefs expounded in the dialogues are those called "serious" above and others like them, and even they reveal mythical aspects. The rest are neither believed nor disbelieved, but occur playfully so that they can be entertained and examined in order to learn what one can from them.

Early in the *Phaedrus*, for example, Socrates refuses to go the way of the "wise ones" (*sophoi*) who explain away the myth of Boreas and Oreithuia. Phaedrus asks if he were "persuaded of the truth of this myth" (*su touto to muthologēma peithē alēthes einai?*). (229c5) Socrates' answer is long and indirect but clearly affirmative. His affirmation of myth in this answer, since it is so resounding and so full of themes which reflect both backward and forward in the canon of the dialogues, can serve as an introduction to the topic of methodology in Plato. As *mythos* belongs to philosophy's pathway (*hodos*), it belongs to its method.

If he disbelieved, Socrates says, he would not be strange (*atopos*), but this task of rationalizing (*sophizomenos*) the myths would keep him occupied with a series of tasks similar to that of rationalizing the Boreas and Orytheia myth. But he lacks the time for such tasks, since they would keep him from the genuinely important task of self-knowledge set by the Delphic inscription. So he accepts the customary view (*nomizomenō*) that the myths are in some sense true. (229c6–230a7)

The Delphic inscription, which itself is a mythical source, requires an unhardened, playful response like the one described above: there are no specific instructions appended to "know yourself." This response plays an important role in the pathway Socrates chooses, directing him away from a path which would require his explaining away the Delphic oracle. Therefore, Socrates' pathway has its origin in myth, and his way of traversing it is governed by the playfulness appropriate to it.

When Socrates says he would not be strange if he disbelieved the myths, he declares his affinity for strangeness. The word "strange" (*atopos*) is also sounded at a crucial point in the *Republic*,[32] and helps characterize the darkness belonging to every Platonic insight. When Glaucon observes that the men in the cave and the images are strange (*atopon*), Socrates immediately answers: "They're like us" (*homoios hēmin*). (515a4–5) The self-appropriation of Socrates to strangeness in his words on the Boreas/Oreithuia myth, and its extension to Glaucon and to the men in the cave, provide a look at the bond of Platonic methodology to darkness.

This strangeness makes itself manifest as a certain orientation to *images*, namely that trust (*pistis*) in their significance discussed above. In the Boreas/Oreithuia case, Socrates never denies that the mythical figures can be rationalized. He merely regards such activity as frivolous for a person who has an important task to perform. In the case of Glaucon and the cave, he never affirms a complete identification with those who cannot distinguish images from their originals. He merely affirms his own bond to images, a bond he shares with them to a noteworthy degree.

In both cases, there is tacit acknowledgement of darkness in the activity of philosophy. Images by their nature are comprised of light and darkness. On the divided line they appear on the bottom, and are said to be "first shadows (*skias*), then phantasms (*phantasmata*) in water and in all close-grained smooth and bright things, and everything of the sort" (*Republic* 509e1–510a2); they are like (*eoiken*) the things they reflect. In interpreting the images as the darkest of the light/dark configurations presented on the divided line, one may regard the movement up the line as an ascent toward the light, away from that which is mixed with darkness.

But the first words of Book VII call such a straightforward view into question: "next, then, I said, make an image (*apeikason*). . ." (514a1) These words occur *after* Glaucon affirms his understanding and arrangement of the divided line proposed by Socrates with the forms (*eidē*), which are the putative truth of images, on top.[33] This imperative for image-making, together with Socrates' affirmation of his own bond to images (that is, to the shadows [*skias*] on the wall in front of the cave-dwellers), suggests that this ascent is far less straightforward and more problematic—more strange—than it may have appeared.

In fact, nowhere in the *Republic* is the ascent enacted. On every occasion when it is discussed with any intensity, Socrates stops short of the top. Either he employs some pretext, such as suggesting to Glaucon that the latter is not quite bright enough to follow; or he employs language suited to the bottom rather than the top of the divided line, such as giving the whole truth as it *appears* to him. (533a1–6 features both dodges)[34] On the other hand, turning points in the dialogue have a way of occurring far from the arguments, in dark places: under the earth with the ancestor of Gyges (359b6–360b2), under the earth where the three metals and their bearers are forged (414d1–415b7), under the earth in the cave (514a1–518c3), and under the earth in the tale of Er which closes the dialogue (614b2–end). These myths are not mere breaks in the argumentative action or means of conveying rational material. They are internal to the methodology and doctrine of the dialogues. The myths function much in the way that the images function on the divided line and the shadows function on the wall of the cave. But this function is properly understood as that primal provocation into and out of the dark from which all philosophizing takes its departure and to which it returns, not as providing an inadequate first step toward clarity and intelligibility.[35]

To say this another way: the dark makes itself manifest in every orientation toward images, whether these images are inspired and complex myths or are the simplest copies of what appear to be the most mundane originals. Even those parts of the dialogue which (as I have said here, and will show clearly in the next chapter) problematically ascend beyond images and hence beyond the dark to pure light contain a recoil to images. The problematic attainment of pure intelligibility always involves a giving over (or at least a giving back over) to the dark.

This bond to the dark makes the kind of seriousness belonging to firm positions inappropriate. Every "position" contains a dark spot, which often makes itself manifest as a scruple which encourages self-questioning (e.g. it is better to admit ignorance then to feign knowledge), or a qualification regarding its ultimate trustworthiness (e.g. the many uses of "probably," "as it seems to me," "presumably," et al.), if not a self-undermining feature (the divided line, which shows knowledge free from images but which is itself an image[36]). Platonic play occurs as the giving over of the soul to the play of light and dark which comprises the field of human attention. Far from abolishing such positions, this play allows them to be held with an appropriate seriousness, i.e. with a rigor and conviction appropriate to their nature, which issues in part from darkness.

In this sense, both doctrine and method originate from and respond to the same partly dark source, and bear the traces of this darkness even (and perhaps especially) when they seem clearest. To regard "doctrine" and "method" as separate in Plato is to miss their common and abiding provocation and source.

Much contemporary Plato scholarship seems at least puzzling when viewed in this light. Terence Irwin and Stanley Rosen, two excellent scholars with apparently quite different orientations, will be treated in order to illustrate this puzzle with respect to methodology. Although Irwin refers to the passage which calls the prisoners in the cave "like us," he misses its significance as Socratic self-reflection, adding casually ". . .and like most people in all cities."[37] Irwin believes in an ascent from image to forms which is perhaps laborious but is nevertheless discernible. For Irwin, the moral beliefs of the many are first criticized by *elenchos*, then are clarified but left incomplete by hypotheses which are thought (but do not rise to principles). By means of dialectic they finally reach their completion (and go beyond moral beliefs) in intelligence. Intelligence then begets "the general theory" which "will be the first principle justifying hypotheses, showing how they fit the teleological account, and at the same time justified as the best synoptic account (531c6–e5, 537b8–c7) of the hypotheses."[38] This ascent is tied back to the *Meno* and the so-called "Theory of Recollection," in the sense that "moral knowledge is reached by learning that uses the learner's own resources."[39]

In his interpretation of recollection, Irwin skips the myth entirely, proceeding directly from Meno's question attacking the possibility of inquiry at 80d5 to the slave boy encounter (Irwin's first citation is 84c10–d2). In so doing, he not only disregards the tale of Persephone but also the crucial establishment of a common ground in the dark of speaking Greek. (82b4) Socrates ascribes the myth to those, such as Pindar, who have been inspired by the gods, and locates the places of sight both in the realm of darkness

(Hades) and of light ("the soul. . .having seen all things that exist, whether in this world or in Hades, has knowledge of them all. . ." [84c5–7]) Recollection is presented not merely as a 4–step process, but also as a process which may proceed out of "one single recollection" if one is strong and courageous. (81d1–4) The myth presents what I will call a vertical account of the ascent to knowledge, accounting for the sudden flash of insight amidst the feeling of thoroughgoing ignorance; the question-and-answer session with the slave boy presents a horizontal one. But the result yielded by the horizontal way is partial even on the level of hypothetical knowledge: the length of the diagonal recollected by the boy is incommensurable. Its precise measure is dark.

Still more important than the epistemological status of the geometrical knowledge achieved is the turning point of the recollective process, the point at which vertical and horizontal meet. This is not the more-or-less successful ascent of the slave boy from ignorance of a certain trigonometric property to knowledge of it, but from the entirely successful recognition of ignorance which made this discovery possible: "By god, Socrates, I don't know." (84a2)[40] Having reached the limits of his ability to calculate and to form plausible answers from these detached calculations, the boy is thrust into the dark. His invocation of the gods may not seem like the one Socrates ascribed to the inspired poets, but it is akin in the sense that it is a giving over to the dark in order to seek an appropriate measure for useful human activity. Irwin misses all of this because he is attuned exclusively to the arguments, which he treats as divorced from the play—including its mythical dimension—to which they belong.

Stanley Rosen pays much greater attention to the mythical, poetical side of the dialogues than Irwin, whose interests lie elsewhere. Both philosophy and poetry "in their conventional identities are quarrelling about the best human life," but it is much too simplistic to say that the one gives truth while the other only images (since in the city in speech given by Socrates no one has the insight to make that distinction). Their partiality provides mutual measuring, the former seeking a kind of knowledge (*epistēmē*), the latter a kind of pleasure. "Philosophy without poetry, exactly like poetry without philosophy, is immoderate or unmeasured. In the last analysis, there is no quarrel between philosophy and poetry." He even calls the "demiurgic discourse" of the dialogues "philosophical poetry."[41]

There is much to commend in such a reading of the dialogues, since the poetical, mythical parts are allowed to contribute freely to the interpretation. They serve as complements to one another, providing clues which might otherwise be missed. Where Irwin found a collection of arguments and paid little or no attention to the myths, Rosen finds a rich intertwining of rational and non-rational elements and discerns a development from the quarrel between the rational activity of philosophy and the darkly inspired poetical/mythical side to their reconciliation.

These two approaches to Platonic methodology, which I have selected for their clear and clearly opposed positions, each yield their measure of results. But methodology was never itself treated in the dialogues or the letters. Even instances of the word *methodos* are relatively few. When "*methodos*" appears, it simply means "procedure," "means to an end" in the most commonplace fashion[42]. The word was used only in particular, narrow situations and by no interpretive stretch could it be applied to the dialogues either individually or collectively. Why is this so? It is difficult to say, but Plato's remarks in the *Seventh Letter* may offer a clue: "when anyone sees anywhere the written work of anyone. . .the subject treated cannot have been his most serious concern." (344c2–3) Methodologies like those of Rosen and Irwin are serious, but Plato places his own dialogues (and letters) on the side of the non-serious, i.e. on the side of the playful. This extends to the written statement on seriousness, which is also not entirely serious, i.e. the interplay of play and seriousness is itself Plato's most serious, and most playful concern.

In this light, both Irwin's complete expulsion of the dark and Rosen's complete incorporation of it impose more structure upon the dialogues than the dialogues impose upon themselves. The dialogues surely speak back to them and reveal aspects of themselves, but these aspects often occur as non-dialogical and disconnected moments. A brief comparison of their treatment of the ascent from earthly to pure beauty presented in the *Symposium* will illustrate this. Irwin finds that "the progress is elenctic. At each stage the pupil tests his aspirations against his present objects of admiration, and though he was not previously aware of it, finds the objects inadequate to his aspiration, in discovering that the reasons he offers for choosing this object really justifies the choice of something else."[43]

While Irwin's account of the ascent is not entirely without interest, there isn't a shred of textual evidence, either in the structure of the dialogue or in the words spoken, for *elenchos* in Socrates' speech. Socrates is *recollecting* a speech of Diotima, there is no "question and answer." In the speech in question, the word *elenchos* doesn't occur once. Nor is anything resembling a formal argument proposed. The mythical and daimonic nature and subject matter of the speech is made clear at the outset and throughout. Irwin's admittedly "speculative" reconstruction uses such mealy-mouthed words such as "reasonably," "naturally," "he will want to," and "he will come to,"[44] to show the key transitions of the ascent; one trembles to think what an *elenchos*-minded Socrates would do with such formulations.

More in keeping with the Platonic text, Rosen observes that "Diotima offers no arguments to support any of her contentions."[45] He concludes by noting that the ascent does not require the body as a starting point (*Erōs* is a very good guide, but there may be better ones for better people), but the ascent to the form (*eidos*) of beauty can begin from the body (taking into account the presumably less exalted denizens of the *demos*). Socrates, who would enact this ascent and empower others to do the same, has both options. Erotics, which are demonic rather than elenctic guides, lead souls upward through visionings of ever truer beauty, as the speech indicates. But Rosen has a problem with Alcibiades, who Socrates seems to love for moral reasons alone: he is "prevented by his *daimonion* from abandoning Alcibiades precisely because of the young boy's hybris and pleonexia [arrogance]."[46]

Rosen's reading of the Socrates-Alcibiades connection takes us outside the dialogue, when there are ample resources within. Heavy drinking of wine has been banished from the symposium connected with the Dionysian festival, making it something less than a complete symposium (*sum-pinō*: to drink wine together; also, there was no wine at the divine banquet spoken of at Socrates' speech. [203b6]) Diotima's speech proceeds as if humans were not earthbound, as if they could ascend to the divine unencumbered by the body and its proclivities, needing only the right kind of *erōs*. But this belief is more akin to *hubris* and *pleonexia*! By contrast, the entry of a beautiful and drunken Alcibiades announces a *restoration* of measure, making the symposium a fully human one again, and restoring the full humanity of the once-again earthbound, embodied Socrates.[47]

The question Rosen raises, of whether or not the body is a necessary starting point for the fulfillment of an ultimate vision, is surely an interesting one and is suggested by some of the speeches. But it is something of a red herring when it is seen at play with the other events in the dialogue (such as the ones cited in the previous paragraph). While he surely takes all elements of the dialogues into account, Rosen does not recognize play in its founding and ultimate role. A concealed but implicitly present rational framework dwells beneath all of these subrational or perhaps irrational elements for Rosen. Both the method of Plato and of Plato interpretation consists of trying to interpret the signs of both rational and non-rational elements so that they may be understood in their unity. While there is room for play in his interpretation, it occurs as a means to the achievement of a deeper rational unity and not as itself the dialogical heart.

For Irwin, by contrast, the dialogues' entire interest consists of their rational contributions. His work consists of extracting their layers of discernible arguments both within and without the so-called Plato-Socrates distinction.[48] But both methods of interpretation aim at unpacking this rich mine of reasoning. The play recedes. So while both Irwin and Rosen offer much that is of value, one cannot at times be sure whether it is the Platonic dialogues being interpreted, certain strains in the dialogues, or whether other interests are being superimposed on the dialogues in an effort to make them say things that they really don't say. Nevertheless, there is much to learn from Rosen about the relationship of the rational and poetic elements, as well as about the more general dramatic functioning of the dialogues.[49]

A brief return to the *Symposium* and particularly to the events before and after the entrance of Alcibiades will show what I mean. *Elenchos* is surely a feature of the dialogues (some more than others) and is just as surely employed by Socrates' in the *Symposium* as well. However, it does not occur in the speech involving Diotima. Rather, *elenchos* governs his encounter with *Agathon*. Socrates refutes (*antilegein*) the claim of Agathon's speech that *Erōs* is beautiful and good, and so leaves the man of honor at the symposium in the perplexity characteristic of such recipients of Socratic purification.

Similarly, a kind of philosophical *erōs* is present in the dialogue, but not in the speech involving Diotima. In Socrates' treatment of Alcibiades we hear of a chaste love which aims at the improvement of the soul of the beloved, and which involves the madness characteristic of non-rational love. But this madness issues not from any unfulfilled carnal or even intellectual desire, but from another variant of the Socratic sting[50] which so often is the outcome of an *elenchos*: "He compels me to admit that while I am deficient in many respects, I still neglect myself. . ." (216a4–6), says Alcibiades, who feels ashamed (*aischunomai*) because he cannot refute (*antilegein*) him. Note that neither this love or this madness is associated with an ascent to the forms, but to the proper regard for the improvement of oneself.

But if philosophical *elenchos* sits to one side of this famous ascent and philosophy as measured earthbound erotic madness sits on the other, how can we interpret the celebrated Diotima-inspired speech in a just manner? First of all, it should be located within the *Symposium* as recollected speech of recollected speeches, and as itself a recollected speech.[51] The dialogue also tells us that we are hearing the speech of Socrates in what is (at best) a secondary sense: in the dialogue it is spoken by Apollodorus, and so must be taken together with what surrounds it.[52] Following the *elenchos* of Agathon which establishes what *erōs* is not, the speech locates *erōs* mythically, and as dwelling in a mythical realm: it is a great *daimōn*. Knowledge is one of the high erotic objects, and *Erōs* is not itself knowledge. But knowledge (by virtue of its beauty) is something toward which *Erōs* directs the soul.

Just when things begin to get excessively bright, i.e. when the speech proclaims the knowledge of the realm of the beautiful where one "no longer holds onto images but to truth, because one now grasps the truth. . ."

(212a4–5), the flute girl returns with Alcibiades on her heels, providing the beautiful images and a beautiful body. As indicated earlier, the earthbound beauty which Socrates abandoned at the end of his Diotima-inspired speech propitiously brings the symposium and Socrates back down to earth. And in Alcibiades' speech, the enactment of Socratic *erōs* is shown as attentiveness to oneself and to one's beloved for the sake of the health of the soul: self-questioning, performing one's tasks without regard to danger, even indulging the intensely measured madness of philosophy. In this light, the ascent of *Erōs* is more interlude than doctrine. The brightness of a human love freed from the body crosses over into comedy,[53] which the entrance of Alcibiades exposes. The Diotima-inspired speech is only one element, the primarily mythical one, at play with the refutation (*antilegein*) of Agathon's initial *logos* and with the deed (of philosophical love) which unsettles the soul of Alcibiades.

Thus any concern for the forms and any ancillary theory of them, or for a theory of the ultimate harmony of poetry and philosophy, is secondary. These issues occur in the midst of the play of human *erōs*, which can both inspire and destabilize any theorizing. According to this reading of the dialogues, internal context and structure provide the framework for interpretation. The dialogues provide the material for the determination of their own methodology.

But to speak of a "methodology" in a contemporary sense may be misleading: as was shown from the start and throughout, *mythos* belongs both to the subject matter treated and to the procedures employed within the dialogues. The interpreter must give himself/herself over to the darkness disclosed in both the myths and their "use" if Plato is to be heard, and not some imported scholarly construct of Plato which would seek or feign light where there is darkness. The *methodos* side of "methodology" must, in this way, be heard as the thoughtful, playful negotiation of a pathway whose origin and whose outcome remain dark.

The relation of these internal procedures and issues to one another and to the whole are disclosed playfully in the dialogues. There is no ultimate resolution, nothing to which one could appeal in full seriousness. In the

Symposium, the interplay of the myths, the arguments, and the deeds allow *Erōs* to come forth in an appropriately human fashion, as clearly present and recognizable yet not fully known and not entirely in our control. Always earthbound and sometimes providing transcendence, darkness always belongs to *Erōs*, transparency is excluded. In the *Phaedrus*, which served to disclose the determinative status of *mythos* earlier in this chapter, this interplay is disclosed as belonging to philosophical *logos* itself.

> . . .one must put together every *logos* like (*hōsper*) an animal, having its own body, neither without a head nor without feet but having a middle and extremities, composed so they are appropriate to one another and to the whole. (264c3–5)[54]

Socrates speaks of the necessity of binding the composition of *logoi*, the putative products of reason, to the image of an animal body. Corporeality, with its thoroughgoing finitude, is prescribed as the model for speech which would convey truth and wisdom. When *logos* is what it "must" be (*dein*), it is already at play with its kindred other, with *mythos*.[55]

In the *Phaedrus*, everything offered to the soul is offered mythically; *logos* and *mythos* are always intertwined. For the purposes of this chapter, a brief treatment of the Theuth and Thamus myth (which will be explored more fully in Chapter 9) will exhibit the nature of this mythical offering. According to this myth, the introduction of writing would ultimately harm memory since the written marks would make recollection (*anamimnēskomenous*) from one's own unaided powers of soul unnecessary. Writing is merely a drug (*pharmakon*) for recalling (*hupomnēseōs*). (274d4-a5) The recollective process is provoked by writing, which is considered here as a non-rational means toward a desired end. It is a means born in myth, possessing powers which are often misunderstood. Once again, the dialogue is indicating how it is to be read.[56] Also, insofar as all of the dialogues are written and that the origin of writing is given in a myth, the dialogues one and all have a mythical heritage included in them.

The "desired end" is nothing like a theory of forms (or any rationalist/intellectualist ethical theory predicated upon it *à la* Irwin) nor an ultimate harmony between poetry and philosophy (the harmony of reason and pleasure *à la* Rosen), but human wisdom and the ongoing pursuit of it. This end is already present in the dialogues which seek it: the play of the dialogues occurs both for the sake of philosophy and from its very nature, and one enters philosophy through the measure-giving play made manifest in the dialogues. Issues like those surrounding the forms and surrounding poetry's role surface and recede; arguments of many kinds, myths, events, jests all have their part. Some of them can be and have been followed through fruitfully when detached from their setting in the dialogue, and developed as full-blown theories or as parts or steps toward them. But this is methodologically derivative at best. Primary is the steady and constant orientation of the Platonic dialogues toward darkness, and this always means toward myth with its components: images and the darkness belonging to their shining. It is an orientation born of the ignorance which gives rise to it as well as the desire for illumination which it seeks and moves toward but never fully attains. The dialogues turn toward that which thwarts the conceit of an intellect that thinks it knows what it does not and thinks it acts upon a firm foundation when it does not. It does all of this not primarily through trenchant *elenchoi* or through superb insights, though these are surely present, but by the playful philosophizing which gives rise to them and measures them.

The playfulness of the Platonic dialogues will not let anything harden into a doctrine by which all opinions are measured or a method by which all cases can be treated. All human claims appear in and against a mixture of darkness and light, i.e. against a certain image-play. Earlier, a healthy orientation toward images was called "trust in their significance"; this attitude toward them was called "strange" (*atopon*) by Socrates. We are now in position to look more closely at this strangeness. The rationalization of myths was called customary. It would be far from strange to say, for example, that the Boreas/Oreithuia myth had its origin in a strong wind blowing a girl off a cliff. In this customary way, the mythical imagery is reduced entirely to natural causes. But the men in the cave on one side, and Socrates and Glaucon on the other are akin in that the images themselves are granted significance, apart from the causal nexus to which they might be ascribed. This trust in the significance of images removes them from the customary and makes them strange, although in different ways.

A-topon literally means "without place" or "having no place" or perhaps "out of place." Socrates, Glaucon and the men in the cave "have no place" in the realm of custom, in the city. Nor have they access to original truth in "the place beyond the heavens" (*ton. . .huperouranion topon*) (*Phaedrus* 247c3), where there are presumably originals free of images, but which is closed off to them (except for glimmers) by virtue of the darkness to which they are given over. Nor are they yet members of its counterpart, Hades, a certain demonic place (*topon tina daimonion*) (*Republic* 614c1), where one finds images (shadows) without originals (real being).

In the realm of custom and opinion, questions regarding the relationship of images and originals, or of appearance and being, are treated as straightforward and as settled: originals are actually existing (sensible) things and their images are reflections or copies of them. In the enslavement of those placed in the cave, in the place beyond the heavens and in the place beneath the earth, these questions do not come up at all. Only where human beings are situated amidst the play of images does the question of their significance arise, and can we encounter them playfully, e.g. inquire regarding their meaning, or follow them out so that they show whatever they can, or put them to a test. Exiled by nature from those places which would either guarantee or foreclose direct access to originals, human beings are given over to images. Trust in images as significant serves as a stand-in for confidence in original truth. Images at play are stand-ins for the well-ordered originals which (we suppose) would provide all that we lack.

The dialogues recollect this bond to images even as we make progress in our inquiries and even seem to transcend this bond. By virtue of the playful comportment toward this image-play, the field upon which the dialogues occur is a rule-governed but open one. Myth with its darkness brings measure just as does *elenchos* (on the side of method) and form (*eidos*) (on the side of doctrine). But play allows them to keep themselves and one another in appropriate accord within the human soul.

CHAPTER THREE:
PLAY AND BRIGHTNESS:
INTELLECT AND KNOWLEDGE OF BEING

As darkness is associated with ignorance, brightness is associated with knowledge. One general way of characterizing philosophy is to regard it as the overcoming of ignorance through knowledge. The remedy consists of distrusting the evidence of the senses and relying upon the intellect, perhaps the intellect alone. This view, sketched broadly here in order to include the widest possible range of options within it, is called intellectualism. Plato is often given credit or blame for it, and his dialogues are interpreted in its terms.

The forms (*eidē*) are intrinsically the brightest of all objects, as they are the correlates of being. They are known through intellect (*nous*), independently of any connection with sensation. The intellection of the forms has been one of the central issues of Plato scholarship, based upon what seems to be unimpeachable textual evidence. But regarded in terms of the play of the Platonic dialogues, this "evidence" can cut in other ways.

So, do we have an adequate grasp of the fact—even if we should consider it in many ways—that what *is* entirely, is entirely knowable; and what in no way *is*, is in every way unknowable?

Most adequate. (*Ikanōtata*)

(*Republic* 477a2-a5)

One could hardly wish for a clearer statement of what has been called Platonic intellectualism. The precisely equal proportionate accord between knowing (*gnōsis*) and being (*on*) is presented as one and the same from whichever perspective it is beheld. It is resoundingly agreed upon (*ikanōtata*) by Glaucon, one of Socrates' most loyal and best students. It appears to presage the three striking images to follow which form the core of Plato's so-called ontology and epistemology. The sun, the divided line and the cave each point to intellect (*nous*) as measure-giving knower of being, perhaps in somewhat different ways and probably most straightforwardly in the divided line. The coordination of intellect with the forms in its top segment is a decisive moment in the history of philosophy, a moment which retains its force.

But in view of the dialogues' playfulness, this intellectualism is not a doctrine or position but a riddle. And insofar as this intellectualism determines a central line of thought from the time of its inception to the present, this riddle reflects back upon the history to which it putatively gave rise.

The riddle is provoked from within the dialogue, and can be formulated using only materials supplied by the dialogue. One is provoked to ask: why is the doctrine of intellectualism, which proclaims the intelligibility of all being, presented by Plato in *images*? Perhaps sharpening this question in terms of the divided line, the *locus classicus* of intellectualism, one can ask: why is the doctrine of intellectualism presented in terms of the *lowest* rung on the ladder, the one which is furthest from being and from intellect? Looking at the same riddle from the crucial transition from Book VI to Book VII, one can (once again[57]) ask: why, immediately after declaring intellect the highest of the affections (*pathēmata*) of the soul, does Socrates say: "Next, then. . .make an image (*apeikason*)?" Why not simply propose to behold and discuss the forms (*eidē*)?

In the same way that myths bespeak a certain orientation of human thought toward darkness, the forms (*eidē*) bespeak a corresponding orientation toward *brightness*. I will leave the Greek untranslated from here on, both because of the encrustation around the term "form" which has occurred since the time of Plato and which has determined the interpretation of it in a certain direction in advance (i.e. as fixed, somehow otherworldly "essence"); and because the Greek *eidos* (plural is *eidē*) preserves the sense of *seeing* (*horaō*). *Eidenai*, the perfect tense of *horaō*, is a word with no intrinsic connection to any "essence" from any world. In other words, my intention is to return *eidos* to the play of the dialogues. (I will also leave *nous*, the most commonly used word for "intellect," untranslated from here on.)

In this play, the one who knows the *eidos* of something appears to be the one who truly knows the thing, just as the one given over to images appears to be the one farthest from this knowledge. Thus, the images seem quite often to function as steppingstones toward this true knowledge, to be used as means through which one moves from the dim reception of mere shadows to the apprehension of being and conduct of life by the brightness of the *eidē*.

But the dialogue does not permit any answer which claims a merely pedagogical use of the images, according to which the sapient soul somehow leaps from the visible to the intelligible realm, from images and things to their eidetic originals. One need look no further than the context of 477a2 (above) to see this. In the preceding distinction drawn by Socrates between the philosophers and the non-philosophers, the ones who can see the *eidē* by themselves are quickly set aside.[58] These seers, able to behold what is brightest all by itself, are declared and agreed upon to be *rare* (*spanioi*); they are not called philosophers. Strictly speaking, no one is directly called a "lover of the sight of the truth" (the description given philosophers), but the only plausible candidate is the one who "believes (*hēgoumenos*) there is something fair itself and is able to catch sight both of it and what participates in it." (476c9-d2)

Thus, the capacity to distinguish the philosopher from the non-philosopher does not lie in the soul's ability to coordinate intellect (*nous*) with the intelligible "things," but rather in the soul's coordination of the intellect with the corresponding *visible* things, i.e. in its ability to apprehend the *eidē* and what participates in them. Socrates speaks of the ones who see beautiful things but do not hold that there is beauty itself as "living in a dream," while the only one called "awake" (*hupar*) is the one capable of gathering the visible things under the *eidē* in an appropriate way.

There is another side to the sight of the philosopher. Not only can the wakeful soul coordinate the *eidos* with what participates in it, but it can also distinguish the two strata within this double sight. It "doesn't believe that what participates is [the *eidos*] itself, nor that it itself is what participates. . ." (476d2-3) Thus, the double seeing contains within it not only the coordination of visible and intelligible but also the power to discern that one leaves off where the other begins. The interpretive task provoked by the riddle now requires that this clear statement of double seeing as the appropriate coordination of visible/intelligible be put together with the intellectualism proclaimed at 477a2 above, although the two seem entirely incompatible.

This putting together can not occur in doctrinal terms (this would be impossible), but in terms of Socrates' way of speaking about what we have been calling "intellectualism." In a word, Socrates speaks *playfully*. He offers no denial of either pole of what seems to be an inescapable logical paradox. There is every effort both to affirm the crowning importance of the *eidē* themselves and to enact the double seeing of which he just spoke. Socratic speech on this matter sets the *eidē* at play: they are at once declared to be the highest kind of knowledge, but in the very declaration they are admitted to be beyond the compass of human knowing.

Socrates develops an extended account of this knowing based upon a threefold structure of powers (*dunamai*) consisting of (1) knowledge depending on being (2) opinion depending upon that which is brighter than not-being but darker than being and (3) ignorance dependent upon not-being. From 477a6 to the end of Book V he gropes for the correlate of opinion, which is presented as most elusive and finally as the domain of the non-philosopher. But this entire stretch of the dialogue is pervaded by the language of opinion spoken by Socrates. Consider the following passages, all of which occur in this stretch:

> Doesn't knowledge naturally depend on what *is*, to know of what *is* and how it is? However, *in my opinion* {!}, it's necessary to make this distinction first. (477b10-12, emphasis and exclamation mine)

> [of the *dunamai* asserted{!} to exist at 477c1] Now listen to how they *look to me* (*phainetai*). ({!} 477c6, emphasis and exclamation mine)

> Knowledge is *presumably* (*pou*){!} dependent on what *is*. . . (478a5, emphasis and exclamation mine)

> Hence, *as it seems* {!}, it would remain for us to find what participates in both—in *to be* and *not to be*—and could not be addressed as either purely and simply, so that if it comes to light, we can justly address it as the opinable. (478e1-4, emphasis and exclamation mine)

The many assertions made by Socrates toward the close of Book V are derived from this opinion-based distinction between knowledge/being, ignorance/nothing and opinion/betweenness. In this light the final passage of Book V, which proclaims an absolute division between the philosopher and the non-philosopher based upon this distinction, hardly settles the question of who the philosopher is. Rather, the question is sharpened and deepened.

In Book VI, both the arguments and Socrates' way of speaking radicalizes the question of intellectualism, which is now bound to the question of who the philosopher is. In addressing Adiemantus' suspicions of philosophical deception and of the viciousness, uselessness and weirdness of those who linger in philosophy, Socrates says: "The question you are asking. . .needs an answer given in an image (*eikonos*)."[59] (487e4-5) After Adiemantus chides him on this, Socrates replies: "At all events, listen to the image so that you may see still more how greedy I am for images." (487e7-488a2) The verb which characterized the philosopher's comportment toward being at the end of Book V was "delight" (*aspazesthai*—479e10); here, the philosopher's defense of his calling by means of a comportment toward images is called "greed" (*glischros*). How can a philosopher, who delights only in the grasp of being by the pure intellect, declare a greed for images?

The sun, divided line and cave hardly answer these new formulations of the riddle of intellectualism. Rather, they extend it further and eventually transform it. The three are at once images which present the way being is imaged in the realm of the visible, and they are images themselves which can be seen as belonging to the same imaging-relation they present. Just as the dialogue seems to work against itself in the undermining of the intellectualist position articulated by Socrates through the speech and activity of the same Socrates, these three images collapse in upon themselves through elements internal to them, as Sallis has shown.[60] The sun image seems to exhibit the intellectualist position most directly: the good grants intellecting and what is intellected in the intelligible region (*tō noetō*)(508c1), a realm entirely separate from the visible. But the image turns in upon itself: the soul, which "intellects (*enoesen*) and knows and *appears* (*phainetai*) to possess *nous*" (508d6; emphasis on "appears" is mine), is said to move between the two regions as if they were not distinct at all but continuous. Apparently at will, the soul can move back and forth between the bright noetic region and the non-noetic region which is "mixed with darkness." (508d4-9) In this light, the soul can move between philosophy and non-philosophy without any difficulty, and so can become either philosopher or non-philosopher depending upon where it happens to fix its look.

The image of the divided line, which follows that of the sun, reflects this continuity. But at the same time, the divided line contains its own internal disruption. While images and imagination are on the bottom as farthest from being and intellect, the divided line is itself an image—and images are located at the bottom section of the line. Further, as mathematical entities apprehended by thought are second highest, the divided line as *mathematical* image cannot account for *nous* and *eidos*, as the line itself does not attain either.

The words which begin Book VII announce the death of intellectualism as a self-sustaining and defensible doctrine, and with it of the view of philosophy as an activity of the intellect beholding intelligible entities: "Next, then, I said, *make an image (apeikason)* of our nature in its education and want of education." (emphasis mine) I propose that the reason for the startling recourse to images here, immediately after the divided line discussion has declared intellect as the highest affection (*pathema*) of the soul, is this: in the *Republic*, it is not the case that images and the realm of the visible generally are beneath the intellect. Rather the intellect and its corresponding *eidē* are functions of the image-play to which the philosopher by nature is given over. The philosopher is the one who is greedy for images, as Socrates has said. In the *Republic* it often appears that the image for which the philosopher is greediest of all is the *image of intelligibility*.

How can intelligibility, with its pure brightness, be classed with darkness-bearing images? As we will shortly see, no claim is ever made, nor is an instance ever given, of a purely intellected *eidos*. The region inhabited by the *eidē* is always presented in analogy with reflected images: (1) the sun yoking sight and what is seen in the visible region is reflected in and analogically related to the good yoking intellect and what is intellected; (2) the divided line extends upward to the *eidē* beyond all lines; (3) the cave culminating in "the vision of what's above [likened to] the intelligible place." (*thean tōn añō tēn eis tōn noeton topon*)(517b4–5) There are junctures at which the intelligible region reflects certain kindred images in the visible; these junctures are the only points of access to the intelligible for human beings. In this sense, even the purely intelligible region (*to noeton*), supposedly free of images by its very nature, is bound to images.

Thus the dichotomy between the philosopher as knower of perfect being free of images and the philosopher as covetor of images is redrawn as the philosopher who strives for *nous* beholding *eidē* amidst the image-play to which human beings are given over. Socrates asks Glaucon to make an image of our nature because an image of it is all we have. He says that the prisoners of the cave are "like us" (*homoios hēmin*)(515a5), a comment that can only mean that we are by nature bound to images from birth, destined always to return to images despite the most dramatic ascents. The image of the cave presents an ascent not much different from that of the divided line; 517a8–b5, where Socrates discusses the cave in terms of the visible and intelligible regions, conforms in large measure to the divided line's segments. The principal difference, as Sallis has pointed out, is that the way up is not continuous but fraught with obstructions.[61] I add that the "they're like us" passage turns the cave image in on itself as well. While in the myth the one released from bonds is shown as exiting the cave and as beholding the truth, Socrates' "they're like us" suggests that no one exits the cave, including the cave's own image-maker. Thus, the exit from the cave, like the ascent of the intellect it presents, occurs only in speech, only as a function of the image-play of the philosopher greedy for images and delighting in intellect as the ultimate image at play.

What is the epistemological status of this ascent? Socrates ratifies its mythical status with recourse to mythical measure: "a god doubtless knows if it happens to be true." (517b6-7) The rise from the bondage of images to the *eidē* free of images, itself given in an image, is consigned to a status far inferior to the knowledge of which it speaks. Socrates' next sentence, in which he celebrates the ultimate vision of the idea of the good as the cause of all rightness and beauty and of all public and private thoughtfulness (*emphronōs*), begins with: "This is how the appearances appear (*phainomena. . .phainetai*) to me. . ." (517b7-8)

The intellectualism of which Socrates seems to speak in Book VI of the *Republic* is never enacted in the sections which seem to be present solely for the purpose of illuminating it; nor is this intellectualism enacted elsewhere in the dialogue. There is not a single instance of *eidē* attaining *eidē* through *eidē* (511b2–c2), nor is there anything approaching a claim that this has been or will be done, nor is a clear instance of upward-moving dialectic provided. There are all sorts of playful dodges, characterized by assertions that the way of discussion being followed is somehow inappropriate for this ultimate ascent, or by disclaimers such as "at least as it looks to me" attached to weighty pronouncements. The passage on dialectic at 533a1–6 contains just about all of these playful evasions:

You will no longer be willing to follow, my dear Glaucon, I said, although there wouldn't be any lack of eagerness on my part. But you would no longer be seeing an image of what we are saying, but *the truth itself, at least as it looks to me. Whether it is really so or not can no longer be properly insisted on.* But that there is some such thing to see must be insisted on. Isn't it so? (emphasis mine)

In this passage, the most exact way to what is clearest of all is presented in the language of semblance and skepticism. The insistence upon some sort (*toiouton ti*) of pure seeing (*idein*) is an assertion of some sort of intellection, but this is hardly the ringing clarity sounded in the passage proclaiming the perfect knowability of perfect being cited earlier in this chapter. The pure seeing of pure truth is given over to imagery and its language, even as Socrates speaks of transcending them. But this two-fold showing is nothing new in the *Republic*: it issues from the twofold image of the philosopher given in Book V (1) as having a double sight with respect to the visible and (2) as concerned entirely with intellect and being.

So the so-called intellectualism of Platonic thought is shown in the *Republic* to be a mere offshoot of the bond to images. Far from pure knowledge of pure being, "intellectualism" is a function of the bond of human knowing to the visible. This bond provides the material and provocation for both this "doctrine" gleaned from it and for the language of Socrates in playfully imparting it.[62] Compared to the belief that *nous* knows the *eidē* independently of sensation, this insistence on the bond to images is in far better harmony with the Socratic ignorance of the *Apology* and the other dialogues in which express acknowledgement is made that one knows nothing regarding anything of real importance.

But what then is the role of intellect? What is the role of the apprehension of being as it is in truth? And who is the philosopher spoken of in Book V, who "delights in each thing that is itself" [480a11] and who has nothing to do with opinion? Clearly, Socrates is not such a philosopher. He says as much when he (1) differentiates the true from the false philosophers by putting those who despise all bodily things on one side and those who do not (485d10–e1) on the other, but (2) was on his way to a feast/festival before being waylaid. Nor is the intellect the actual affection (*pathēma*) of the human soul which really apprehends the *eidē*. Rather, it is precisely what is present as missing from the powers of human thought as it strives to satiate its desire for knowledge with actual knowledge.

Intellect, pure knower of pure being, is the name given to that power which we precisely do not have, just as being in itself is precisely what we would but cannot know. Intellect and being can only be grasped in *logos*, but never brought forth purely in deed. However, this does not make them insignificant at all, but merely relocates their significance in such a way that they serve their appropriate function in proper measure. What has been called intellectualism has the crucial function of measuring human thought by showing where it cannot go (and therefore where its proper domain lies). It is the source of all of the playful dodges, all of the language of semblance in the *Republic*, all of that part of philosophy which remains aware of its own limits. It is an imagined extension of the limited but definite power of thought in the realm of the visible (the double-seeing), an image which would leave its source in the visible behind and forgotten. . .if matters are taken too seriously.

In this sense, to speak of a Platonic ontology is to speak of something present as lacking, as a *necessary* lack. This absence of intellect, being and their coordination—this lack of clear signposts, clear guides—is why the soul must undergo great labors through its own in darkness (including, but not only the dark of the cave and of the "certain demonic place" seen by Er) in order to find a suitable city for itself. And this is also why a certain comedy attaches to those labors: the city it would build must be fashioned out of elements from the same region (the visible) using the same imperfect means (thought bound to imagery) from which the soul must protect itself.

But this city, as Book IX shows at its conclusion, "has its place in *logoi*" since, as Glaucon says, it is not found on earth ("unless some divine chance coincidentally comes to pass"). (592a7–b1) Socrates replies that perhaps (*isōs*) its paradigm is available in heaven for the one who wishes to found such a city, and that it doesn't matter whether the city exists anywhere or not. The man having *nous* will mind this city which he founded in speech, and no other. Thus, the man of *nous* will ultimately guide himself in terms of something fashioned in speech *for which there may be no paradigm anywhere*. Nowhere in the *Republic* or in any other dialogue is a way given to interpret heavenly paradigms, nor does the aforementioned divine coincidence occur.

So the one having *nous* is not said to fashion his city in terms of pregiven, fixed *eidē*. The paradigm they would provide either exists nowhere, or perhaps where there can be no guide to its interpretation. The one having *nous*, then, must build his city in speech through play, just as Socrates has done in the *Republic*. The cities in speech built in Books II-IV were driven by images and myths connected to the work required in cities. The reflective enhancements upon the "just" city in Books V-VII are also shot through with playful elements, as Part II will show. These cities and the reflections upon them are surely serious as well, but they are functions and outcomes of the most profoundly searching play.

Again, none of this is to suggest that *nous* and the corresponding beholding of the *eidē* is not a major theme in the Platonic dialogues. But since *nous* never occurs except insofar as it is at play with seeming, appearing and the other ways of apprehension associated with sensation (*aisthēsis*), it cannot be said to take place purely. Even the representation of *nous* as separable is parasitical upon the sensation it purports to leave behind. Nowhere is this more striking than in the *Phaedo*, where the separability of *nous* from *aisthēsis*, and with it the entire activity of philosophy, takes place only in the face of death.[63] Philosophy in this living world (presumably employing *nous* to its fullest degree) merely provides practice, says playful Socrates. (67e4–5)

Ironically, it is the connection with death which most clearly and forcefully brings out the role of *nous* and the *eidē*, especially their connection with their most valued quality and most often mentioned associate, truth. On the one hand, disembodied *nous* is said to be coordinated perfectly with the *eidē*, and after death this coordination will be experienced by the true philosopher. But in this life, the bond to sensation (*aisthēsis*) impedes the experience of this perfect coordination and thus keeps the philosopher from pure truth. But even here, there is a dodge: "And in this way, freeing ourselves from the foolishness of the body and being pure, we shall reach the company of those like us who know things through themselves and purely: that is presumably (*isōs*)(!) the truth." (67b1) And this dodge is shortly followed by another: "Then, Socrates said, *if* that is true, my friend, I have hope. . ." (67b7–8)

The story from the embodied side is rather different. After discarding Anaxagoras' conception of *nous* on his first voyage and despairing of finding some other teacher (97b8–99d2) who can teach him how *nous* is the cause of all things, Socrates turns from the attempt to behold beings directly (fearing excessive brightness which would blind him) to beholding them in *logoi*, which he both likens to and distinguishes from *images* (*eikona*). Like images, the *logoi* reflect beings indirectly; unlike images, *logoi* reflect them accurately (see 99d4–100a3) and make it possible to apprehend them so that one will not be blinded by them.

> Then I lay down (*hupothemenos*) in each case the *logos* I judge to be healthiest (*errōmenestaton*), and whatever seems to me to agree (*sumphōnein*) with it, I set down (*tithēmi*) as true.
>
> (*Phaedo* 100a3–a8)

This *logos* consists of the *eidē* of which he has always spoken: "the beautiful itself according to itself, and the good and the great and all the rest." (100b1–8) No more mention is made of the coordination of *nous* with *eidē* which was so celebrated earlier in the dialogue. If anything, *nous* is here to be feared as exposing the human soul to a brightness its nature is unable to bear, a brightness that would endanger its sight.

What does the Socratic recourse to *logos* mean? The negative significance could not be clearer: for humans, there is no direct access to being in this life (and to speak of other lives is to speak in terms of *mythos*, or what is most removed from this direct rational beholding). To say this in the language of the divided line, there is no ascent to the highest segment of the line. To assess this recourse more directly is to encounter its strangeness: what agrees with the *eidē* is true, but what makes the *eidē* the touchstones of truth is neither their clarity nor their self-evidence but their healthiness, their vigor: the *eidē* are the principal constituents of the healthiest, most vigorous *logoi*, and so for Socrates they are truth's standard.

Perhaps it is not so surprising to find truth drawn up in terms of a splendid body. After all, on the day of his death, the most "noetic" of humans was found practicing music, the exemplary practice of and for the body. And the agreement with an *eidos* which makes a hypothesis true, according to Socrates, is given in musical terms (*sumphōnein*).

What makes the *logoi* of the *eidē* most vigorous is the service they perform in argument for Socrates, who either persuades or enrages his interlocutors with them. The *eidē* must be assumed in some form to account for various acts of knowledge, or at least for the attentiveness (*apoblepsis*) necessary for coherent experience. (cf. *Parmenides* 135b5–c3) Precisely because they cannot be beheld directly, they must be argued either for (this makes them the healthiest) or from (this makes them touchstones of truth). It is their absence from our embodied gaze that brings fear of death as fear of what is unknown. Their imperfect, indirect presence in *logos* gives courage and hope to one who, like Socrates, can trust *logos* as a human being's best guide, although it may be second-best in the catalogue of possibilities generated by the play of images.

This trust is felt in the body. The accord of an insight with the *eidē* is *heard*: the agreement (*sumphōnein*) has the sound of harmonious music as well as the assent of thought. In this way, philosophical *logos* becomes first of all the sweetest music in the play of sensation (*aisthēsis*), and only then does it become a source of theories and doctrines. What, then, becomes of *nous*? Far from being the pre-eminent faculty of human knowledge, it becomes a playful image, a part of the human struggle to know and to give a name to what is closed off to it. In this capacity, it surely names a region to which we have some limited, indirect access (in *logos*) and so holds an honored place in the Platonic dialogues. But insofar at it is never actually enacted, this place and its honors cannot be inhabited or even described—except at play, in images. As serious possibility, *nous* belongs to the dead.

CHAPTER FOUR:
PLAY IN THE MIDST OF ORDER:
DISRUPTIONS (DARK AND BRIGHT)

The Platonic dialogues feature frequent shifts of topic, interruptions of one interlocutor by another, eruptions of speeches and events which provoke a turn in the proceedings, quieter and more subtle shifts which redirect the discourse, sudden exclamations, and other disturbances of the seemingly smooth progress of philosophical exposition in conversation. I call such occurrences *disruptions*, and regard them as intrinsic to the dialogues' way of philosophizing. No one who reads the Platonic dialogues, even superficially, can fail to note these peculiar interpolations, the likes of which are seldom if ever found in other philosophical writings. But they belong to the play of the dialogues in important ways, breaking in when matters are on the verge of becoming brighter or darker than appropriate to the measure of human insight.

Just as the dialogues' arguments and myths belong to that primordial play which is most appropriate to the human soul's nature as both bound to images and as attempting to transcend them, so the disruptions in their midst disclose the play which animates them and introduce their own measure into the activity of the soul. In this sense, the disruptions occurring within the dialogues disclose the dialogues themselves as disruptions of the soul's customary habituation. Even those dialogues which may seem most straightforwardly to be proclamations of a certain view (e.g. *Menexenus*)[64] or refutation of a view (e.g. *Laches*)[65] break up what is supposed to be a clear surface of firm belief, and upon inspection prove to have heterogeneous elements within them that threaten to disrupt not only their blindly accepted surface but also aspects of themselves.

In terms of the previous two chapters, disruptions are manifest as eruptions of darkness into what had previously seemed like bright surfaces and eruptions of brightness into what had previously been dark surfaces. They are never presented as philosophical positions or as premises or conclusions of arguments, but as intrusions which break up the apparent flow of the discourse and seem to redirect it. In the deeper movement of the dialogue, however, these disruptions are precisely what the discourse requires. They are playful in the most fundamentally Platonic sense: by shaking its foundation, they restore measure to a section of the dialogue which might otherwise have become inappropriately serious in some way. I will look at this phenomenon in two of the three dialogues treated in the previous chapter (*Meno* and *Symposium*), and conclude with an interpretation of the *Parmenides* which will reflect back upon the developments both in this chapter and in Part I as a whole.

Many refutations by cross-examination (*elenchoi*) in the *Meno* suggest themselves as disruptions, upsetting previously uncriticized beliefs. Meno's initial inability and later ineptness in the art of attentiveness (*apoblepsis*) beget three rapid and devastating refutations of his definitions of virtue from Socrates, and the supposedly aporetic conclusion of the dialogue can be seen as exemplifying philosophy's supposedly negative, critical function. But there are other disruptions which are not formal *elenchoi* but which disclose essential issues present in the folds of the express arguments about human virtue. Meno asks, quite directly, whether Socrates thinks virtue is taught, comes through practice, comes by nature, or is acquired in some other way. To Meno's "multiple-choice" question, a Socratic "essay" is the response.

This Socratic response comes nowhere near the express content of Meno's question on the genesis of virtue, and so disrupts the flow of what looked to be the beginning of a standard-fare exchange of opinions on a matter of frequent and casual debate. It begins by praising Larissan and Thessalian horsemanship, continues through a clear reference to Meno's connection with Gorgias and an allusion to Meno's good looks, and concludes with a profession of thoroughgoing ignorance about the subject of Meno's question. (70a5–71a8) Far more than a textbook example of Socratic irony, this response is designed to disrupt Meno from his habit, and discloses one requirement for a proper approach to the question of virtue.

Such an approach requires actual contact between the soul of the questioner and its subject matter. Within the response, Socrates says, ". . .I admit and accept blame (*katamemphomai*) that about virtue, I do not know (*eidos*) anything: and how, if I do not know what something is, can I know how it comes about?" (71b2–4) The strange words seek to shift the discourse from the genesis of virtue, a theoretical matter which distances virtue from the speaker, to the form (*eidos*) of virtue, which raises the question of its actual presence to the questioner's soul as a living issue. They declare personal responsibility for the treatment of the issue. The Socratic disruption brings the *eidos* nearer to human concern than it was in Meno's question, makes it brighter than it was as a mere confused and uncritical opinion.

Meno has his turn, too. After having been refuted in all his attempts to define virtue and all his efforts to recall what Gorgias told him about the nature of virtue, he calls Socrates confused, ugly and disorienting to others (at 79e8-80b7). After failing to provoke Socrates with this *ad hominem* attack, Meno disrupts Socrates' elenctic practice with his question on the possibility of knowing:

How will you look for something without in the least knowing what it is?
How are you going to set up what you don't know as the object of your search?. . .How will you know that what you have found is the thing you didn't know? (80d5–9)

While Socrates disparages this clever-sounding but supposedly empty question, it nevertheless transforms his practice in this dialogue: Socrates takes recourse to *mythos* for the first time, and to demonstration (*apodeixis*) for the first time.

The myth of recollection and encounter with the slave boy were interpreted in the previous chapter, in terms of the appropriate darkness they introduce. It is enough to say here that in terms of the dialogue and its outcome, they are not merely means of instruction for the doltish Meno but essential ways of showing. By contrast to the negative result of Socrates' interrogation of Meno, they introduce a measure of light. The myth and the encounter are alternative to argument not merely because of Meno's recalcitrance and/or stupidity but because as argument breaks off (here, in the attempt to define virtue[66]) other ways of showing enter.

The event which redirects the way of showing is Meno's attack upon Socrates and his self-undermining question upon the nature of inquiry. These disrupt the interrogation of Meno and provoke both the myth and the demonstration which secured the possibility of inquiry, results which the elenctic process did not accomplish on its own. At the time of the disruption, both Socrates and Meno are in the dark regarding knowledge of virtue. Only through a myth of Hades and through a geometrical demonstration which passes through many errors and culminates in an incommensurable outcome—that is to say, through disruptions of the argumentative process—does Socrates point toward the (bright) possibility of education and toward the discovery of virtue. Meno's question, disparaged as an "eristic *logos*" by Socrates (80e2), provides the disruption which calls forth the crucial philosophical insight.

This crucial insight is nothing other than the awareness of lack of insight. It attains its odd fruition after another elenctic interlude, another explosion of frustration, and another image of Hades. Anytus believes than human beings receive virtue from their fathers. But after agreeing with Socrates that Aristides, Thucydides and Themistocles are good men, Anytus concedes that the sons of these men lack virtue. (93a5–94e2) When challenged to admit what this concession entails, namely that virtue cannot be taught, Anytus threatens Socrates and leaves. (94e3–95a4) This threat, issuing from the implication that Anytus was a virtue-lacking son of a virtuous man, is carried through in the accusations reported in the *Apology*. In terms of the *Meno*, the inappropriate seriousness of Anytus reveals an inability to entertain the issue of virtue in proper measure, and the negative answer to the question leaves the interlocutors at a loss for a clear answer.

The enthymematic conclusion is that (*contra* one of the so-called basic tenets of Platonism) virtue is not knowledge.[67] Socrates then leads Meno to concur in the view that only by inspiration (99c3–4) do such virtuous people obtain virtue, since they were not taught nor were they born with it. Inspiration and divine dispensation (99e6—*theia moira*) are ways of saying that the advent of virtue is dark, unknown. The reference to Homer's words on Tiresias in Hades, "he alone is wise (*pepnutai*), the rest are darting shadows" (100a5–6; *Odyssey* X, 494) makes this vivid: Tiresias can see best of all in Hades, but he is irremediably blind. He "disrupted" Athena, gazing upon her accidentally while she was about to bathe. Athena "disrupted" Tiresias in return, taking his sight. But then she granted him the gift of prophesy and a walking staff. Once having seen the goddess of wisdom naked he was closed off from the vision forever. The myth suggests that mortals are not to have uncovered truth revealed to them. But even without this direct sight of truth—within the darkness to which he is irrevocably given over—Tiresias can make his way quite well.

So the pathway to wisdom and virtue is shrouded in darkness, blocking direct access. Yet Socrates closes the dialogue by insisting that he and Meno must still ask the question "what is virtue?" One can surely understand how this ending, together with the lack of any answer, has marked the *Meno* as an "aporetic" dialogue. However, this reiterated and apparently unanswered question should be seen most fundamentally as affirmative, i.e. as a repeated and healthy disruption of our habituation. It is only secondarily the conclusion of a somewhat misdirected effort of inquiry. Far more, it provokes the recollection that virtue involves a certain orientation to the dark, a reminder that we do not know in any originary or firm manner and so need to question ourselves as a matter of course. In this sense the question "what is it?" (*ti estin*), to which a clear theoretical answer is absent, is itself disruption out of habit and opinion and into the darkness which must be acknowledged as belonging to our domain.

This question also opens up a correspondingly bright region which also belongs to our domain. The act of questioning directs one toward that sighting (*eidos*) which may not be granted directly but which is accessible indirectly, and serves to measure human action even without its full presence. In the deepest sense, there is no confusion (*aporia*) at the end of the *Meno*. Virtue is not defined, but much that is clear has been discovered. Virtue is not many and relative (72a1–5); it is not defined as "ruling men" (73c9–d1) or as "the desire for beautiful things and the power of acquiring them" (77b2–5); nor is it acquired by teaching or by nature. Socrates rules himself throughout these "discoveries" in the dialogue in terms of what he knows and what he doesn't. In so doing, he distinguishes his activity from that of Meno and Anytus, who lack but profess confident knowledge. When confronted with their ignorance, they threaten and attack. Socrates lacks confident knowledge, but acts in a measured manner. His confidence issues from a willingness to confront ignorance, from his determination to live well while dwelling partly in the dark. Thus, there is a glimpse of virtue in his activity and bearing: virtue is seen as the power to rule oneself in a way which accounts for both one's knowledge and one's ignorance. No fear of disruption is present, for that would mean fear of discovering ignorance. This fear would be fear of brightness as well as of darkness, fear of a challenge to the habituation which flattens them out into the comfortable gray of received opinion.

In Chapter 2, the *Symposium* interpretation illustrated the way method in the dialogues was bound up essentially with darkness. We return to that dialogue again here because it is the one in which disruption most obviously penetrates the proceedings. Not only do disruptions occur all over, but disruption itself is thematized throughout. The title announces that drinking of wine will occur, but the participants banish the usual heavy wine drinking from the occasion and also the flute girl (176a4–176b10), causing a decisive turn which shapes and, in a way, distorts the speeches. A still more decisive turn occurs when wine is reintroduced after Socrates' speech.

(213e12–214b1) Both, we shall see, are disruptions, and both disruptions are formative influences upon the philosophical "positions" articulated in the dialogues.

Even the structure of the *Symposium* speaks disruption: its main character, Apollodorus, did not hear the collection of speeches he has rehearsed thoroughly and aimed to recite accurately. Rather, he learned them from Aristodemus (172b8–173b6), who forgot much about the speeches, including (presumably) his own. (178a1–3) And we learn early that narrator Apollodorus, whose desire to celebrate both the occasion and the activity of philosophy which informed it, had his life disrupted by it and sought to disrupt others as well. (173c1–174a1) Aristophanes' hiccups first disrupted the serial order of the speeches, then disrupted the speech of Eryximachus which proclaimed love as the harmony of loves within the body. (185c4–d5,189a1–6)

In the midst of these disturbances, confident accounts of love are given. Love is bound to honor, especially in the face of death (Phaedrus); Love can and should be made subject to human law (Pausanias); Love is a harmony of opposites (Eryximachus); Love is the desire for (recovered) wholeness (Aristophanes); Love is the desire for (direct) goodness and beauty (Agathon); Love is a great spirit, between gods and men, a longing for the permanent possession of the good. This possession appears to be accessible through an ordered ascent from love of a beautiful body to love of pure eidetic beauty (Socrates). It is customary to look at the speeches prior to Socrates' as partial accounts of love and as somehow anticipating their appropriate incorporation in the Socratic *tour de force*. But even these prior disruptions suggest that the Socratic speech, by virtue of its clear solution of the "problem of love" through its ordering of loves under a single characteristic, does not truly transcend its predecessors but belongs together with them.

The speeches of men who have chosen to be sober, moderate and sane for this occasion speak of Love as if forgetfulness, drunkenness and madness could be overcome by it. They proceed as if the wine-god could be absent from Love's true nature as easily as they could choose to banish the flute girl and take a night off from heavy drinking. Especially in the speeches of Socrates and Agathon, the body and its claims are treated as if they could somehow be overcome in human love. From the hiccups of Aristophanes to the Socratic *elenchos* of Agathon[68] (199c3–201c9), which perhaps is Socrates' speech properly so-called; from the various occasions of discord and negativity within the speeches[69] to the more general and comic negativity that no one has previously given speeches in praise of Love (177a3–d5)—all of these suggest not merely that the mere attempt to bring love to *logos* is disrupted because of some human frailty, but that disruption itself belongs to the nature of human love and so always finds itself included in *logoi* which seek to give its measure.

So it is not merely that human *logos* bungles in its attempt to speak worthily of love. Love itself exercises a disruptive effect upon human *logos*. In other words the madness, drunkenness and forgetfulness, which threaten to disorder the speeches and which the men would banish at the outset, are in fact essential to them. The very existence of the speeches, whatever sense they make in the effort to order them, and whatever sense they fail to make—these issue from Love. And those disordering phenomena occurring within the speeches suggest that their supposedly external counterparts are hardly alien to them. Disorder belongs to Love as much as order, this disorder (this *alogia*) cannot be banished: so says the second half of the *Symposium*, beginning with the entrance of Alcibiades.

The sudden intrusion of Alcibiades is a peculiarly Platonic event in the play of the dialogues: a disruption which is entirely measure-restoring[70]. Socrates' speech concludes with praise of love of pure beauty "not contaminated with human flesh and color and a lot of other mortal silliness." (211e1–3) Then Alcibiades as the one beautiful body (the lowest rung on love's ladder) enters, with the previously banished flute girl and attendants. This entrance playfully complements this all-too-divine Socratic speech with Alcibiades' (and Socrates') all-too-human flesh. In Nietzschean terms, the introduction and the speeches present the Apollinian aspect of the symposium in its well-ordered orientation toward completeness and goodness with respect to the beloved, and in so doing they make manifest a necessary aspect of love. But this aspect is not, by itself, sufficient.

The entrance and speech of Alcibiades provides the previously expelled and missing Dionysian aspect. His initial encounter with Socrates (which declares Socrates' orientation toward the best-looking) and especially his making drunk of the participants destroys the order of the speeches. While his roaringly earthy entrance undercuts the lofty conclusion of Socrates' speech, he reintroduces an order appropriate to a human symposium. Such a gathering must pay appropriate homage to the things of the earth, i.e. to wine, to women, to music, to garlands from plants worn about the head. In this way, Alcibiades serves as the restorer of order through his deed of disrupting the proceedings. The previous order, in which the things of the earth were denied in service to a sober reading of love, was a sham order. It disserved the disordering essence of *Erōs* and its tie to the earth.

Socrates, the rational refuter of Agathon and the proclaimer of disembodied *Erōs*, is called one of the Sileni and also called Marsyas the Satyr. (215b4–6) These Dionysian images are far removed from the serene truth-and-goodness seeker of the first part of the dialogue. Although encouraged to if he finds them untrue (214e10–11), Socrates raises no objection to these images being ascribed to him. Socrates is depicted as the most provocative disrupter of all, turning Alcibiades' soul toward goodness and driving him mad in so doing. Virtually everyone who comes in contact with him is provoked not nearly so much by his reason as by his strangeness (215a2—*atopian*), by the profound disruptiveness of his darkly working practice. Unsettling disruption of the soul lies at the heart of its erotic orientation toward the order that is best for it.

In the *Parmenides*, one hears echoes of the dramatic structure of the *Symposium*, of the formal elenctic structure of the *Meno* and of the disruptive features of both.[71] As in the *Symposium*, the impeccably accurate narration of a speech heard long ago is at issue. Again, the speech comes complete with precise interpolations, although none of the original speakers are present. In the *Symposium*, Apollodorus is "not unprepared" (*ouk ameletētos*) (172a1), based on his hearing it from Aristodemus and rehearsing it; in the *Parmenides*, Cephalus heard it from Antiphon, who also is "well prepared indeed." (*eu mala diemeletēsen*—126c8) Aristodemus the teller recorded no speech of his own, just as Pythodorus, who taught the speech to Antiphon, did not speak. This distance between speaker and speech impinges upon—disrupts—trustworthiness, making possible what is at best a partial trustworthiness. But again, this partiality is as far as possible from a defect. As both dialogues show, a partial trustworthiness of human *logos* is appropriate to philosophy,[72] as is the recognition of some kind of ineradicable darkness at its heart.

In the *Parmenides*, the disruption of age and youth is layered onto the disruption signalled by the distances in the telling of speeches. Within the recollection, the passage of time has found the once philosophically-zealous Antiphon occupied with horses, and reluctant to recall the recalled conversation. (127a1–a7) And within the recalled conversation we find Parmenides reluctant to engage in the greater exercise (*gumnasai*), likening himself to "the old race horse in Ibycus, who trembles at the start of the chariot race, knowing from long experience what's in store for him," then to an old poet who has fallen in love and fears love's rigors. (136e9-137a3) Both of these images disrupt: a philosopher describes the strength of his powers to attain what wisdom he can as proportionate to the strength of his body, not as deriving from the efforts of his soul.

This disruption recalls the tie of philosophy to the body which was exhibited in another way in the *Symposium*. The Socrates/Alcibiades tie is echoed in the Parmenides/Zeno tie, although somewhat more quietly. Zeno (who is 40 years old) is described as tall (*eumēkē*) and graceful (*charienta*), and is said to be the favorite (*paidika*) of Parmenides (127b4–5); Parmenides' bearing is called noble and good. Socrates chides Zeno who sought, with his book, to associate himself with Parmenides in writing as well as in friendship (*philia*). But Zeno affirms both bonds quite calmly. So love in the *Parmenides* seems less aligned with madness and drunkenness than love in the *Symposium*, conditioning the apparently more unified and homogeneous focus of the *Parmenides*. But the disruption at its heart is the same, and so is the way this disruption generates the outcome.

At stake in the argument are the *eidē*, and the rigorous gymnastic conducted by Parmenides and undergone by Socrates reaches an aporetic conclusion. In a crucial sense, the gymnastic designed to empower Socrates to find truth functions as yet another disruption, in the face of which both the defenders and attackers of the *eidē* seem helplessly perplexed. The *Parmenides* can be seen in this light as yielding a far more sophisticated and more general result than the *Meno*, which dealt with one *eidos* clumsily but reached a similar conclusion with respect to knowledge.

The *eidē* are not treated as if they were actually beheld as detached from and instantiated in the things in which they are said to participate. (Nowhere in the Platonic dialogues is such a beholding ever claimed.) In the *Parmenides* they occur primarily as the correlate of focused, attentive vision (*apoblepsis*). Just as Socrates tells Meno at 72c8 that the one who would answer the question of what virtue is would do well to have his attention fixed (*apoblepsanta*) however many and different the virtues are, Parmenides tells Socrates that if someone won't admit that the *eidē* exist or won't distinguish a definite *eidos* in every case, he will not be capable of attentiveness (*apoblepsas*) in his thought and will destroy the significance of all discourse (*dialegesthai*). (135b5–c3)

What disrupts the attempt to experience the *eidē* as they are in themselves? Two answers suggest themselves at once. (1) The ever-present bond to the body denies complete knowledge of complete being. (2) Argument itself is vulnerable to *elenchoi*, and thus produces confusions which undermine the effort at clarity. The actuality of the tie to the body, which precludes originary experience of the *eidē*, is the correlate of the confusion-begetting arguments of the *elenchoi*. But in spite of these disruptions, the *eidē* reinsert themselves anyway, out of the need to fix our gaze attentively in thought and to speak intelligibly to one another and to ourselves. Even *erōs* can be seen as arising from this need, as the way of human union in the face of the partiality attaching to all attempts at genuine insight into being, and to all orientations toward goodness and completeness.

These three quite different Platonic dialogues are driven not by theories or even by attempts to construct theories but by what is almost their opposite. The *Meno*, the *Symposium* and the *Parmenides* are driven by disruptions of many kinds which put to rout any attempt to establish the orderliness of a theory, finished or otherwise. The responses to the disruptions are not solutions or returns to order, but thoughts and actions which honor the darkness out of which the disruptions arose as they bring to light what human insight can attain. There is no ultimate answer to the questions of virtue, love or the *eidē*, and the recourses to ordering by means of them are given over to myth (or to a mythical kind of fogginess in the *Parmenides*). In other words, the disruption remains in force.

But in the same way, disruption lights up the atmosphere in which it occurs in distinctive ways. In the *Meno* it indicates the need for a perpetual return to virtue (*aretē*) as a question for one who would live well. Virtue is not given in any intellectual formulation. The *ti estin* ("what is it?") question is not settled in this way at all, thanks largely to the disruptions. But virtue remains open as a task for the seeker, as a veiled but discernible image to be lived through.[73] Similarly, *erōs* is never defined in such a way as to close off discussion. Even the body-transcending conclusion of Socrates' Diotima-speech (211d1–212a7) is playfully refuted by the demonstrated love of Socrates for beautiful-bodied Alcibiades. Here the disruption clears the way for the image of a human love that neither ascends to the *eidos* of beauty nor binds itself to the human body. Rather, this love is shown in the appropriate care of one's own soul and of the soul of one's beloved. Also similar is the interplay of the bodily image in the *Parmenides*, i.e. its gymnastic, with the intelligible *eidē*, the subject of the discourse. The outcome is the fruitful confusion (*aporia*) by which the *eidē* remain necessary for human thought even though they are not ultimately known.

In all three cases, the outcome is neither knowledge of the *eidē* nor some derivative. Nor is it blindness and random groping, nor self-serving sophistry. The dialogues have yielded a measured response to the distance experienced by human beings from knowledge and from goodness. Directly and indirectly, they seek the best arguments, the healthiest *logoi*,[74] available. From this seeking, previously undiscovered routes can be found. Insights are one and all corrigible, always at play. But nothing is loose or arbitrary, the play of the dialogues has rules of its own which are discovered only through the ongoing struggle to know the truth and to act well. Far from undermining supposedly more serious aspirations, the play of the Platonic dialogues allows dimly glimpsed and not truly known originals to function as ruling images (e.g. the forms, love, virtue) which both provoke and guide human life, even as it denies the originary insight which would make us more than human.

None of this is particularly interpretive or tied especially to the "dramatic" side of Plato. It is built both into the philosophizing on the "issues" and into the interaction between the elements and the personages (as if one could draw a line between the two!). This mixture of distance from and guidance by originals is in perfect accord with Socratic ignorance, and with the ever critical and ever affirmative image of Socrates presented in the *Apology*. The playfulness of disruption is a major aspect of the enactment of philosophy in the Platonic dialogues. It makes philosophy's vision manifest together with the limits of that vision, presenting its order together with the undermining of that order. The openness of inquiry, the willingness to admit and to confront ignorance, the frequent recourses to non-rational sources, the lack of firm philosophical commitment to any theory or doctrine but only to ongoing honest questioning, the willingness to enact and to undergo disruption—in one phrase, the play of the Platonic dialogues—provide a unified discipline and rigor which gives measure to all of its putatively more sophisticated, less playful successors.

PART II

PLAY AND THE CITY

CHAPTER FIVE:
PLAY IN THE CITY

The Platonic city—what is it? Where is it? At the outset of Book X of the *Republic*, Socrates refers to aspects of "this city" (598a2), meaning the city in *logos* spoken of at the close of Book IX. This is the city which, as we have seen, may have its correlate only in heaven and does not, it would seem, exist anywhere on earth. In any case, its existence somewhere "doesn't make any difference." (592b3–4) In other words, the city which Socrates is most concerned with founding and investigating is undetermined (at best) with respect to its existence. But its ontological status does not matter. It is a city at play.

The fashioning of this city runs through the issues of education and poetry, but before introducing them we will take our departure from Book II of the *Republic*, where the matter which drives the discussion first arose. In this way the city can be traced from its origin in genuine human concerns and human wonder. Adiemantus and Glaucon are puzzled, having heard justice praised by most people as a mere compromise and injustice regarded as preferable were there no possibility of punishment. They wonder about the worth of the justice they still somehow prefer, and wish to hear Socrates praise it both for itself and for its advantages. The search is undertaken by means of investigating justice in a city, such that something smaller (justice in the soul of one man) can be seen in something bigger. (368c4–369a3)

Thus, the cities in speech by means of which the interlocutors would try to see justice are in service to the remediation of genuine human ignorance and confusion regarding a matter of great importance. But how are the cities in speech fashioned? Precisely the way that actual cities come into being, out of the non-self-sufficiency (*ouk autarchēs*) (369b6) of each individual. All cities have their origin in human needfulness and incompleteness, whether they are cities in speech in service to answering basic human questions about justice or whether they are actual cities.

The task is to see how this is so and to see how these needs are met, so that justice can be seen. Almost all of the verbs Socrates uses throughout the inquiry suggest sight in some way: "observe closely" (*rhaōn katamathein*) (368e8), "seek out" (*zētēsōmein*) (369a1), "observe" (*episkepsōmetha*) (369a1–2), "consider the *idea*" (*episkopountes*) (369a3), "behold" (*theasaimetha*) (369a5), "see" (*idoimen*) (369a6), "see" (*idein*) (369a9), "seek" (*zetoumen*) (369a10). The sighting called for is a reflective sighting, which gleans something about the act of seeing from what is seen. This capacity for reflective sight will prove to be central to the political discussion.

The end of Book IV bears this out. Now that the likeness of city to individual human being has been accomplished such that the three classes of citizens (guardians, auxiliaries, artisans) are proportioned to the three parts of the soul (calculation, spirit, desire) with each part minding its own proper business, Socrates calls the vantage point to which the argument has elevated them a "lookout" (*skopias*—445c4), and the verbs of sight recur: "see very thoroughly" (*kateiden*) (445b6), "see" (*idēs*) (445c1), "behold" (*theas*) (445c2). But the journey from the early groping to the final lookout is fraught with turns which not only shape the journey and its outcome in unsuspected ways, but which also transform the apparently unproblematic reflective seeing which guides the journey. Two transformations occur on the way of this journey, one to the "city/individual soul" likeness and another to the reflective sight which investigates this likeness. As we will see, these transformations converge in a peculiar way.

The first crucial turning occurs at 372c2, where Glaucon begins to redirect the conversation from Socrates' first city of artisans to a second city of luxuries. The first city disclosed the rule of "one man, one art" (370b1–3) and revealed justice as originating from the need each human being had of the others and of the whole. The second, luxurious city not only cannot sustain these principles, but cannot function at all as a place where justice can be sighted even in speech. This is not merely because Socrates will not consider whether war, which is necessary to attain and protect the luxuries, "works evil or good" (373e4–5) (although one might certainly wonder how a discussion of justice can take place while abstracting from a crucial matter of good and evil). It is because the nature of the guardians, who will wage war and who will acquire and protect the luxuries, brings forth the presence of *injustice* in an unavoidable way.

By nature, the guardians "must be gentle to their own and cruel to enemies" (375c1), and their entire education (to be discussed below) is geared toward the fashioning of such a human being. But these qualities, gentleness to one's own and savagery to others, echo the ones proposed in Polemarchus' earlier definition of justice: helping one's friends and harming one's enemies. (332d7–9)

But this is a definition which Socrates clearly rejects!

In an exchange from 332e1–335e10, Polemarchus himself gradually backs off from his original opinion that justice is helping friends and harming enemies, opting in the end for a partnership with Socrates in the belief that it is never just to injure anyone. Yet this rejected combination of helping/harming is the aim of the education of the guardians in the luxurious city. Thus the emergence in *logos* of the guardians, who must in this light be considered as *images of injustice*, changes the status of the investigation of justice. In such a city in speech, we can only find justice (in whatever measure it is present) mixed with a profound injustice at its origin and at its core, in its founder and in its guardians. Recalling the parallel, the individual soul must likewise find justice and injustice present together at its origin and core.

By an indirect but discernible path, the discussion recalls the confusion in the souls of Glaucon and Adiemantus which gave rise to it. They found men praising justice for its reputation, but preferring to do injustice where they could do so undetected. But the desire for luxury (gain) and the desire for justice cannot coexist: this is one outcome for the soul in the consideration of the guardians by Glaucon, Adiemantus and Socrates. So long as there are guardians educated to help friends and harm enemies, injustice dwells at the core of the city according to the argument of Socrates in Book II. Thus, the reflective sight sees no conformity between city and soul in terms of the *idea* of justice, but only a disconformity between a clear argument offering an aspect of justice ("never harming anyone") and the most important part of a city in which justice is supposed to be glimpsed (the "harming others" of the guardians). In other words, the reflective sight is brought forcefully before the justice it does not see.

Still further, the education of the guardians, whereby they learn friendliness toward their own and savagery toward others, is undertaken in a way which seems designed to implant injustice. It is the way of rigorously regulating what those most spirited youths will see and hear, of lying to them when it would serve the interest of the city, and of censoring those often traditional materials which stimulate emotions and practices deemed disadvantageous to the city's interest.

But it is as clear as anything in the Platonic texts that the education of the guardians is undertaken in a spirit of *playfulness*. Socrates announces the governing status of this playfulness at the outset: "Come, then, like men telling tales in a tale and at their leisure (*en muthō muthologountes te kai scholen agontes*), let's educate the men in speech." (376d9–10) In a sense they are all already at leisure: they are engaged in philosophical dialogue far from the affairs of the city. But the leisure and its implicit freedom is constrained by the needs of the city in speech they are founding, just as the setting of the dialogue was determined by a certain constraint from the outside, the playful "force" of Polemarchus (including the promise of a torch race on horseback and an all night festival) which brought Socrates to the house of Cephalus. (327b2–328b3) At least in a general way, there is a limit on the realm of play which is set by these constraints.

This declaration of playfulness by Socrates and its accompanying question allows this discourse to go forward both within and about *mythos*. With respect to content, the musical part of the education of the guardians consisted primarily of the traditional myths of Greek culture. It is well known that in his treatment of these myths Socrates says he will censor some, alter others, and excise others entirely. Recalling the declaration of playfulness, we find that it entails *en muthō muthologountes*, mythologizing like men in a myth. Thus the playfulness already involves a mythical orientation toward *mythos*.

What can this mean? In a straightforward sense, it means that the proposal to regulate the making of myths is not itself serious. This should not be surprising at all, in light of the injustice at the heart even of the conception of the souls of the guardians. Nor is it surprising in light of the nature of the mythology to be censored/altered/purged. Homer and Hesiod appeal to and acknowledge the Muses as their inspiration. The tragedians Aeschylus, Sophocles and Euripides draw upon this traditional material, and their work is performed at the festivals which bear the name of Dionysus and which celebrate the power of the gods. In all cases the mythical material occurs within a form which acknowledges the non-human origin both of the material and of the poetic inspiration at the source of its presentation. Thus, Socrates' claim that the *mythos* should or even could be subject to human control or regulation cannot be entirely serious, but must be playful in important ways. This playfulness is indicated by its leisurely presentation which is itself given over to *mythos* and which is presented by men in a myth speaking mythically and playfully about the most serious matters.

Two such matters are intertwined in the education of the guardians. One concerns the appropriate design of the city (*polis*), which we would today call political philosophy (although there is no such locution in Plato). The other concerns the appropriate education of the individual soul, which we might today call poetics with dashes of ethics and psychology.[75] I maintain that neither matter occurs as truly serious in the dialogue, that no positions are taken regarding either one in the dialogue, and that there are prominent play elements which clearly signal this non-seriousness and non-positionality. With respect to the city, this element is the *philosopher-king*; with respect to poetry and the individual soul, this element is the apology[76]/chanting (*apologia*/*epōdēn*) exchange. After the functions of these elements are established, we will be in a position to look at the matters of "political philosophy" and "poetics" in relation to the city in a fitting way.

> 'Unless,' I said, 'the philosophers rule as kings or now those called kings and chiefs genuinely and adequately philosophize, and political power and philosophy coincide (*sumpesē*) in the same place. . .there is no rest from ills for the cities, my dear Glaucon, nor I think for humankind, nor will the regime we have now described in logos come forth from nature, insofar as possible, and see the light of the sun.' (473c11–e1)

The verb announcing the nature of the joining of philosophy and political power is outrageous, almost ridiculous: *sumpesē*, from *sumpiptō*, which means "to fall together" as if by accident, or to collapse together.[77] After the rigorous regulation and censorship of what the guardians will hear, after the most austere proscriptions upon what people can own and can call their own, after the most careful control of who will mate with whom—in other words, after top to bottom governance of all aspects of social and political life in which all aspects of chance are excised—we are told that such a city cannot come into being at all unless some happy and extremely unlikely accident, outside of all human control, somehow occurs.

But even to call this a slim hope is to overstate its possibility. Let us examine what the *Republic* presents about each part of the term "philosopher-king." At 485c3–4, Socrates says the following about those having a philosophic nature: "[They have] no taste for falsehood; that is, they are completely unwilling to admit what's false but hate it, while cherishing the truth." And after a bit of play culminating in Glaucon's admission that there is "no way" the same nature could be both a lover of wisdom and a lover of falsehood, Socrates says (with apparent redundancy), "therefore the man who is really a lover of learning must strive as intensely as possible for every kind of truth." (485d2–3)

This almost overbearing emphasis upon the philosopher's unswerving orientation toward truth and corresponding hatred of falsehood serves to distinguish him absolutely from the political ruler, to whom falsehood is clearly necessary. The ruler must use many drugs (459c2–3), among them "a throng of lies and deceptions for the benefit of the ruled" which have utilitarian value "as a form of remedy (*en pharmakou eidei*)." (459c8–d1) The most dramatic lie of all with respect to the city has already been told: the noble lie, which arose "of need (*en deonti*)" (414b9), and which told the guardians and rest of the city that their education and rearing had itself been a lie.

The layering of lies on the political side is thick and dauntingly complex: the initial mythologizing within a myth which undermines the traditional *mythos* issues in a great lie for the sake of the remedy of concealing a throng of lies told for the sake of a remedy. In any case, the nature of the politically powerful is not only distant from the nature of the philosophical, it is clearly antithetical. The two cannot be reconciled in any way; one can never admit the other without destroying its own essence. There can be no "falling together," even by the most extraordinary chance.

How, then, must we understand Plato's astonishing conditional? Regarding it as the major premise of a hypothetical syllogism, and determining the truth value of each part in terms of what the text of the dialogue has yielded, the radical incompatibility of the philosophic and political natures means that the antecedent is true: the philosophic and political natures will not "coincide." Thus, the consequent is true also: there is no rest from ills for cities or for humankind, and the city which is the outcome of the education of the guardians will not come into being.

The optimistic parallelism suggested at the outset, according to which justice seen in cities was to serve as an aid to the sighting of justice in the soul, turns out to have a darker side. This darker side could not be put more starkly: just as cities will never be free of ills (*kakon*), souls will never be free of ills. The reflective sighting which appeared so direct in Socrates' earlier admonition now requires the recognition of dark spots within it: just as the one who would behold justice in cities must also see these ineradicable ills, the one who would behold justice in souls must see them there as well.

But this parallelism is not total. Looked at either from the bright side (according to which the parts of the city directly image parts of the soul, and each part's minding of its own business constitutes the justice of each), or from the darker side (according to which cities and souls are both fated to be afflicted by ills), the parallel breaks down at crucial points, even at the end (the close of Book IX). While there is no way for the regime fashioned in speech to come into being, Socrates does not say that such a regime in the soul cannot come into being. More precisely, he says that there is no remedy from ills for souls or cities, but there may be a way for a suitable regime to emerge in the soul apart from the ills of the city. The soul may be able to manage its own ills in a just manner.

This break in the parallel is foreshadowed in the treatment of courage, where Socrates calls "political courage" the power and preservation of the right opinion of what is terrible and what is not. (430c2) This specification of courage as "political" suggests that there is a separate courage of the individual soul unconnected to the opinions required for the running of the city. Here we see how the break in the philosopher-king image reflects the asymmetry of courage with respect to souls and cities. The courage of the philosopher manifests itself in its recognition of ignorance and pursuit of truth, as distinguished from the guardians' unquestioning protection of the governing opinion in the city.

There is also a break within the city in speech itself, which is almost comic given the birthplace in injustice of this city. At its outset, the guardians were educated to gain and protect luxuries. But at its fulfillment, the guardians and their auxiliaries own nothing, and the artisans own only enough to sustain them. The city has been purged of those desires and possessions for the sake of which the education of the guardians was first fashioned. The luxury-gaining/austerity-commanding transformation in the city in speech and the contradiction (the philosopher-king) that its outcome forces is another manifestation of the perpetual instability in the political realm, i.e. of its perpetual engagement with ills (which will be played out in Books VIII and IX).

However, there seem to be no ills in the city purged of luxuries. But this is because the people of this city have been purged of all individual desire, and desire in general has been relegated to the lowest status.[78] The distinction between what is best for the individual soul and what is best for the city has been completely eradicated:

> I suppose, then, that when one of its citizens suffers anything at all, either good or bad, such a city will most of all say that the affected part is its own, and all will share in the joy or the pain. (462d8–e2)

In addition to there being no ills in the city, there is also no playfulness. It has been "educated out" of the souls of the guardians and auxiliaries (who are not even permitted to laugh heartily [388e5–389a7]), and legislated out of the lives of the artisans (who can only own enough to keep them working continually, between luxury and poverty).

And since there is no playfulness, it should be no surprise that there is no *philosophy* in the city in speech. In fact, there is no philosophy either in the earlier version of the city, which was given over entirely to the acquisition and protection of luxuries, or in the later version, which was purged of the desire for them. Since there is nothing but the darkness of sheer desire for plenty in the earlier version of the city and nothing but the brightness of sheer service to its unity in the latter, there is nothing of the dark/light play which gives rise to the wondering and questioning peculiar to philosophy. To be sure, even the first city of artisans (called a "city of pigs" by Glaucon at 372d4 and a "true" or "trusty" [*alithinē*] city by Socrates at 372e6) had no darkness. With each man performing his function and justice originating from mutual need, the first city's basic features are intact in the third, purged city—except that the citizens now residing in the third city have even fewer possessions than did the "pigs" of the first city before Glaucon gave them their luxuries.

There are cracks even in the *conception* of the three cities. In the trusty city, the artisan's art and the wage earner's art are co-present in the same man; thus the "one man, one art" rule is violated. The luxurious city must be purged of luxuries in order to survive. And the purged city is preserved by marriages of the best to the best, "sacred marriages" (458e3) (i.e. Zeus-Hera, brother-sister marriages) which would eviscerate the "best" stock at least as certainly as the outlawed mixing with the lower classes.[79] Thus, the cities in speech themselves, despite the apparent effort to craft them as serious proposals, display a comic element. Their very conception and elucidation, i.e. their being formed into an image of some distinctness, contain the seeds of their undoing, i.e. of their inner self-contradiction.

Thus, the inner incompatibility of philosophy and political power and the consequent impossibility of the philosopher-king shed a playful light back upon the generation of the cities in speech, and in a sense upon all cities as well. In one sense, the light illuminates gloom and pessimism: there can be no respite from ills in cities. In another, it can be seen as hopeful: the play of good and ill cannot be extinguished, and the individual human soul may in some sense free itself from the ills of the city. The philosopher-king is itself an image of what is at play in the relation between the individual human being and his or her city, whether within or without: the ongoing need for truth, and the ongoing need for ruling images (called "noble lies" here) to impose order and purpose. The two are always at play, and this is why I called the philosopher-king a play element.

The other play element spoken of above, the one connected to poetics, appears in the context of the admission of poetry to the city in speech. After characterizing poetry as beloved and charming, but as nourishing pleasure and imitation rather than what is shown to be best by argument, Socrates counsels that until it makes an appropriate apology "we'll chant (*epōdēn*) this argument as a countercharm, taking care against falling back into this love (*erōta*), which is childish and belongs to the many." (608a2–5) Chanting (*epōdēn*) and arguing (*legein*[80]), the activities proper to poetry and to apologizing respectively, seem to be at odds in Plato in a manner akin to the discord between political and philosophical activities. But unlike the latter clash, chanting and arguing allow for a resolution which reflects upon the entire character of the Platonic dialogues.

Unlike "philosopher-king," the tension between chanting (*epōdēn*) and arguing (*legein*) does not have a contradiction at its heart. The *logos* has dismissed poetry from the city (607b3), and with it the singing peculiar to it. Argument is ruled by reason and poetry by pleasure and pain. But an apology "in lyrics or some other meter" (607d3–4),[81] which establishes the beneficence of poetry in addition to the pleasure it brings, would allow for its readmission into the city alongside argument. This readmission would be welcome: despite the ancient quarrel, Socrates and his interlocutors would be delighted since they are charmed (*kēloumenois*) by it.[82] (607c5–8)

Further, the natures of the philosopher and the king mutually expel one another. The most that Socrates can say (and the enactment of even this remote occurrence is impossible, as we have seen) is that the natures may fall together by chance. But the rigorous education prescribed by Socrates for the guardians has not even been successfully completed by *Socrates*, who *still* loves the same poetry he would expel as dangerous to the well-disposed soul. Still further, the need for chanting the argument as a countercharm strongly suggests that *logos* by itself is not sufficient to regulate poetry.[83]

A chanting of the argument against poetry in order to protect against the childish love of it: what does this say? It announces a playfully poetic encounter with the mighty power of poetry, a power which insinuates itself into the soul through play. And supposedly mature, serious *logos* must give itself over to this childish play in order to compete with it at all. Thus either poetry must chant its apology to be readmitted into the city, or *logos* must be chanted in order to protect itself from a childish love of poetry. The city of the soul, in order words, must always be engaged in chanting.[84] It must always be given over to poetry, music, play. *Logos* always occurs against a prior play, with this play serving at least as its background.

Thus, the discussions of the philosopher-king and of apologizing/chanting remain within the playfulness which serves as its proper setting. The philosopher-king as playful image, exhibiting the possibility of the just city, accomplishes the opposite. It discloses the impossibility of an actual city coming into being along the lines of the purged city which served as the model of justice. The philosophic nature must always be truthful; the kingly nature must sometimes tell great lies. There is no hope for accommodation. The sighting urged by Socrates beholds this anomaly, this darkness. This city in play plays a game with a dark outcome, reflecting the darkness of its birth in ignorance and need.

By contrast, *logos* can accommodate itself to chanting in the individual soul. Truth and proper measure disclosed through *logos* can admit the music proper to poetry with its hedonistic "lies," which are not willing lies designed to manipulate citizens but inspired images fashioned to enchant souls. In the city within the soul, these functions occur as exchanged: *logoi* are chanted in order to enchant souls, poetry sings its apology in order to observe proper measure. In the city within the soul, these opposites at play are its basis.

The existence and non-existence of the best Platonic city may be a matter of indifference. Its ultimate location may not matter, except to the one who would fashion such a city within. Such a city cannot be fashioned externally, as its culminating need for something which cannot come into being—a philosopher-king—makes clear. But the possibility of such a city in one's own soul through the practice of philosophy remains open. The wonder-based questioning of young Glaucon and Adiemantus in Book II of the *Republic*, as well as the mythical representation of learning of souls even after death in Book X, serve as examples of its playful affirmation.

CHAPTER SIX:
MYTHOS AND LOGOS IN THE CITY

When interpreted in light of the play of the dialogues, the existence of a Platonic political philosophy is at least questionable. While the issue of Plato's political beliefs has produced much animated and perhaps fruitful discussion in this century,[85] the discussion presupposes a reading of the dialogues which assumes a serious approach to politics much like that of Hobbes and his successors. Elements which do not belong to rational arguments in our modern sense are ignored or diminished. But in the dialogues, political issues are always at play with others. One separates them out at the cost not only of ignoring this play, but of ascribing views to Plato which can find little or no support in his dialogues.

Speaking not just of political philosophy but of the general orientation of the Platonic dialogues toward dividing philosophy into separate specialties, Sallis recalls the stark textual fact that Plato never said anything in any of the dialogues. He says that

it is highly questionable whether there is any such thing as the philosophy of Plato—that is, whether philosophy as presented in the Platonic writings is such that it can ever be appropriately spoken of in such a phrase—that is, whether philosophy can ever be the philosophy *of* someone or whether, on the contrary, such a phrase does not already betray such a falling from the demand placed on philosophical thought, a falling away in the direction of opinions, which indeed are the possessions of particular men in particular cities.[86]

Both the habit of ascribing philosophy to a person and, by extension, of ascribing philosophy to predetermined regions are called into question not merely by Sallis' fine observation but by the Platonic practice which inspires it.

This practice ascribes no opinions or beliefs to its author,[87] and makes no divisions into regional and separate subject-matters. The way of the dialogues precludes such ascription and division. Further, matters concerning the city (*polis*) always occur amidst other concerns. Some of these concerns, such as the larger issue of justice, belong to our sense of political philosophy and can even be said to derive from Plato. Others, such as the nature of poetry, do not occupy our political philosophy as much though they were certainly of great concern to Plato. Both the issue of justice and of poetry intertwine for Plato in ways which are at least somewhat strange to most of us today, but which we must address if our interpretation responds faithfully to the dialogues. This fidelity benefits our efforts to approach philosophy in a manner appropriate to the dialogues, but incurs costs in an effort to read off a separate political philosophy suitable for contemporary academic needs.

As the previous chapter has shown, the location of the city is itself no straightforward matter. It is seen as residing in actuality, as the place where human beings actually conduct their business, where the whole of human life from birth to death is undergone, and where people are involved with questions of justice and the like. But it is also seen as residing in the soul. Such a city may be inhabited by few, but if it is well-founded, it is the true home of the one who founded it, rather than the actual city. Thirdly, we may speak of cities in speech (*logos*) as cutting across the other two and as, in a sense, distinct from them. In the *Republic*, three cities are built in *logos* from Books II-IV, and four others are presented in Books VIII-IX). Only one (the third, purged city of Book IV) serves as a paradigm for the just city in the soul. At least one of them (the first city, of artisans, in Book II; perhaps also the pure democracy in Book IX) has no counterpart in actuality. The location of the city spoken about at any time is a matter for question, and its various placements frustrate attempts to give a firm foundation to what we normally understand by "political philosophy."

The previous chapter also established that the city occurs most fundamentally as playful in the Platonic dialogues, where it is always first and foremost a city in *logos*. Reflecting elements of the soul, of actual cities, and of their mixture, these cities in *logos* provide a place where the nature of humanity and human activity open themselves up and out into a realm in which they can be seen, considered and discussed. Although in certain manifestations it becomes a place most inhospitable to philosophy, as a city in *logos* at play it is philosophy's friend. Through engagement in dialogue with the cities in *logos* and with their counterparts, philosophy is able to become most fully what it is, even when (and perhaps as especially when) the outcome is the death of the philosopher, as is the case in the *Apology*, *Crito* and *Phaedo*.

In our consideration of the city regarded as serious political unit in this chapter and in Chapter 8 (where the *Apology* will be the principal focus), it should not be surprising that the playful quality of the dialogues will appear to diminish. Several key concerns of "political philosophy"—such as those of political freedom, decisions over life and death, and the regulation of property—seem to exclude the jests and twists and other manifestations of the openness and sheer pleasure in the exercise of human thought and language directed toward what is best. While this seriousness exacts its measure, it cannot entirely suppress the dramatic inversion of what is considered valuable in light of the play.

In this inversion, which Socrates presents in a vivid and vicarious image, the worth of these key political matters diminishes to nothing as the matters affecting the soul are elevated to the status of the sole bearers of genuine worth.

In the *Crito* the imprisoned Socrates, while awaiting death and playfully contemplating escape, declares his fearlessness of the many, even if they "frighten us with even more terrors than at present, as children are frightened with goblins (*mormolupettai*), threatening us with imprisonments and deaths and confiscations of property." (46c3–6) In this passage, the most serious matters of political life are likened to *Mormōn*, a non-existent she-monster used to frighten recalcitrant children. *Mormōn* is a peculiar kind of play entity, an invention employed to manipulate someone in an ignorant and inferior position. Through its power over another's fearful ignorance, a playful and powerful image is in service to a manipulative seriousness. When one leaves childhood *Mormōn* is no longer fearful: one knows that *Mormōn* is an image without any power.

Imprisonment, death and confiscation of property—how on earth are they like *Mormōn*? They are alike in that no one who knows what they are and what they are worth can possibly fear them! Their unreality in relation to what is truly right and good for the soul is like the unreality of *Mormōn* to an adult. In light of the dialogue, the key objects of our political philosophy are the concern only of frightened children. What are freedom, life and property? Childish playthings. One outgrows any love for them when one engages in a life governed by *logos*. But since the life governed by *logos* is a life given over to play at its outset, what is disclosed in the play of *logos* is more binding and hence more serious than the most serious matters of the city.

The image of *Mormōn* is an image for the soul. In childhood, it serves to direct one to observance of proper measure, and uses fear as the directive. For an adult, it is disgraceful to be led by fear of the many and of what they fear. The directive for an adult should be what is right as disclosed though *logos*. The issue of childish fear will resurface powerfully in the treatment of death and the *Phaedo*[88]. But it is clear that this fear persists, and that discovering the means to its alleviation is an important part of the business of political philosophy. Gathering the basic concerns of the city into the vicarious image of *Mormōn* serves to remind the souls of Socrates and of Crito that at the least, there are other directives to human actions than fear, and other aims than freedom, life and property. His impending death, then, offers no grounds for him to "abandon the *logoi* held in the past." (46b6–7) Rather, he hears these *logoi* as the play of the flute music of the Corybantes

(54d3–4) at the dialogue's end.

These *logoi*, free of concern for freedom, life and property, turn out to be the ones which bind him most firmly to the city. These playful *logoi* lead him to remain in Athens and accept the verdict of his city rather than escape, and thus to honor both philosophy and the just claims of the political realm with good cheer.

* *

When the city is considered apart from its occurrence in the play of *logos*, a presentation which is more sober can be expected. One of the purposes of this chapter is to provide such an account of the city in Plato which, in addition to being faithful to the dialogues and given in terms of the guiding point of view of this book, can be compared with other points of view concerning "Plato's political philosophy" and evaluated. But even in such a presentation, it becomes impossible to sustain the illusion that the city of which we speak can be considered in abstraction from the governing dialogical considerations. In other words, we can expect cracks even in the places where the discourse appears most measured and most solid. Both in the dialogue and in its interpretation, where the play is most suppressed it surfaces most forcefully.

A close and serious reading of the Platonic dialogues, especially of the *Republic* and the *Timaeus*, also reveals a tension in the very nature of a city. This tension has nothing obvious to do with those more manifest tensions associated with the task of harmonizing disparate interests within a single unit. Nor is it the overlay of city in *logos*/actual city spoken of above. In a sense, however, it underlies all of these other tensions, and underlies our way of speaking about them as well. *Mythos* and *logos* are inextricably interwoven, but they do not completely intersect: this is the source of that tension, as the Platonic dialogues show in their central passages upon the founding of republics (*politeiai*). This interweaving/non-intersecting of *mythos* and *logos* will take place by means of a synopsis of the issue of myth-making and its attempted regulation in Books II-III of the *Republic*, of the unwitting mythologization in 20d7–26e1 of the *Timaeus*, and a commentary upon the fundamental tension exposed by these synopses. Then, a few conclusions will be offered concerning the way *mythos* and poetic imagery inhabit the more reflective and prosaic language usually associated with political concerns.

In the *Republic*, it appears that for a just city to come into being, *mythos* must be entirely subordinated to the apparently rational aims of the state. In the previous chapter, many playful anomalies were exposed in the education of the guardians. Here we look at the regulation of the subject-matter of the guardian's education even more thoroughly, with an eye on the full impact of Socrates' playful proposal. The subordination of *mythos* to the aims of the state does not merely extend to this or that tale, but seems to go much further: not only are the myths themselves to be supervised and regulated and the myth-makers (*mythopoioi*) made subject to a rigorous set of rules, but also *the conditions of mythos itself* are to be excised by this supervision and regulation. The darkness to which humanity is delivered over and out of which all myths emerge, that darkness which also comprises the central subject-matter of mythology, is precisely what the supervisors will purge from the myths in order that it be purged from the souls of the guardians-in-training who will be the guarantors of the new just city.[89]

The following list, taken serially from Books II-III of the *Republic*, should make clear how thoroughgoing is the purge of dark impulses and actions. Forbidden are:

violation of oaths	379e3 and f.
strife (among the gods and elsewhere)	380a1 and f.
causing evil	380a3 and f.
manyness	380d1 and ff.
lying	382a1 and ff.
	389b2 and ff.
fear of death	386a7 and ff.
crying and lamenting (in general, and for lost loved ones)	387e9 and f.
laughing	388e5 and ff.
disobedience	389e13 and ff.
excess (in general, and in food, drink	389e13 and f.

and sex)

desiring gifts and money	390d7 and ff.
comedy and tragedy (perhaps)	394d5 and ff.
womanliness (boasting when happy/ mourning and wailing when in misfortune)	395d5 and f.
insulting, making fun of, using shameful language to one another	395e7 and ff.
love	396d2
gifted wisdom	398a1 and f.
Lydian and other "wailing" musical modes (and all but military modes)	398e1 and ff.
many-toned and panharmonic instruments	399c7 and f.
meters (rhythms) fomenting illiberality, insolence, madness, vice	400b1 and f.

Taken together, this list would clearly do away with far more than merely faction-causing behaviors and the states of soul which give rise to them. Spiritedness itself would be banned. The same quality of spirit which recommended the guardians to the founders in the first place is ironically and comically being stripped from them. In short, the young men with the most intense spirits are to be told the sappiest myths, and are to sit still for them as for their physically nourishing food. Still further, the myth-makers are to sit still for a method of regulation which contradicts much if not all that is at the heart of what they do.

Chapter 2 presented myths in the Platonic dialogues as providing likely accounts of matters which are by nature deeply veiled, matters which are inaccessible to *logos* understood as a way of giving "rational" accounts. Further, myths serve as bearers of the tradition of a people, keeping alive old stories. "Old stories" here has two senses, both "stories of what is old" and "stories which have been told, in various guises, for a long time." Socrates' prescription to the myth-makers would at least severely injure the first and would destroy the second. But the practical impossibility of the latter signals the provisional and ironic character, i.e. the sheer playfulness, of Socrates' suggestion that the poets be regulated and censored. To expunge the strife of the gods in the *Iliad* or Achilles' loud and mournful lament at the death of Patroklos, or to editorially delete Odysseus' lying in the Odyssey would not merely deform (or reform) these individual myths. Such "surgery" would carve whole pieces out of the Greek soul. There is much question about whether such a thing can be done at all.

But the supervision of the myth-makers has a comic dimension which is still more ridiculous. This supervision tacitly assumes that the poets proceed according to some rational design which can be altered in terms of another (presumably better) design, namely the one of the founders who would fashion the new "just" city. But few matters have been more clearly articulated throughout the Platonic dialogues than the one according to which poets and other artists proceed not by reason but by inspiration (*enthousiastikos*). Their works come not out of knowledge or insight but by means of a gift, out of darkness.[90] Thus the regulation of subject-matter is ridiculous, almost inherently absurd, because the poet (for Plato) simply cannot have control over his/her subject-matter (not to mention the preposterousness of insisting upon inspired works about strait-laced, unfeeling dullards). So from both sides, the side of the subject-matter and the side of the creators of the subject matter, the supervision of myths must be understood as playfully nonsensical.

However, when we invert this absurdity we discover its more serious underside. There is no question that for cities to exist with a modicum of justice, the darker impulses have to be brought to some kind of rule. While the supervision of the poets may be comic in speech and impossible in deed, the need for two kinds of tale is quite clear and reasonable. There is a need for tales which arise out of the darkness of human nature in order for human beings to come to see themselves truly, to recognize and express themselves fully. And there is a need for tales which seek to regulate human behavior for the good of the whole. The two seem hardly incompatible, both in principle and in deed. The word *mythos*, appropriate to both kinds, was in early Greek synonymous with *logos*, and even later had the primary significance of anything delivered by word of mouth.[91] This common origin suggests that the comic task discussed above need not be comic if differently framed, that there can be *some* accord between the needs of a wisdom-seeking human soul and the needs of a city, just as there may be between the *mythoi* which serve each.

But neither the nature nor the degree of confluence are presented as settled, if indeed they are possible at all. In the *Timaeus* we are given, as if it were a completion of the comedy which was begun in the *Republic*, still another comedy in which an attempt is made to render superfluous both *mythos* and the darkness which is both its origin and outcome. If there is a difference, it is one merely of degree and not of kind. The *Republic* treated *mythos* as if it could be entirely subordinated to consciously determined aims in the fashioning of a republic (*politeia*). The *Timaeus* treats *mythos* as if it were a mere aberration dependent upon an accidental circumstance of a people, i.e. as if *mythos* were dispensable in principle and, under good circumstances, in deed as well.

When we study the surface of Critias' speech about Atlantis, we find an apparently straightforward historical account of the Athenian rescue of Egypt several millennia ago from the attacking Atlantans. Significantly, Critias presents his account as "an old *logos*" (21a8) rather than as *mythos*. Further, this account was told to the Critias of the dialogue when the latter was ten years old by the elder Critias, who was ninety years old at the time of the telling. The elder Critias, in turn, heard the account from Solon, who (also in turn) heard it from Egyptian priests. The account, in brief, proceeds as follows: out of *hubris*, the Atlantans planned to attack the whole of Europe and Asia, but a noble Greek people repelled them, and their island was swallowed up by the earth soon thereafter. And most remarkably of all, the city which Socrates thought he had founded merely in *logos* on the previous day (in the *Republic*) actually existed as such in deed those many millennia ago, and was peopled by the same race of Greeks to which Solon, the listener, unwittingly belonged, and which performed the heroic rescue in a manner entirely in keeping with Socrates' account. (21e1–26e1)

This report of what happened millennia ago is offered with serene confidence by Critias, and presumably in the same spirit by the elder Critias, by Dropides, by Solon, and by the Egyptian priest who speaks to Solon with beneficent condescension. Although Critias admits that the lapse of time made him unsure, on the previous day, of the degree of clarity of his account and so he was silent (i.e. at the *Republic*), one night's effort gave him complete recollection. And so Socrates' city in *logos* offered in a mythological context in the *Republic* (i.e. "like men mythologizing in a myth and at their leisure, let's educate [the city's guardians] in *logos*" (376d9–10)) is effortlessly elevated to actuality in the *Timaeus*. Critias, who calls this account of his a *logos*, says to Socrates in the *Timaeus*:

> And the city with its citizens which you described to us yesterday as in a *mythos* we will now transport into truth, and posit that the city is that ancient city of ours, and that the citizens you conceived are the true progenitors of ours, of whom the priest told. (26c7–d3)

This "transportation"[92] (*metenegkontes*) is empowered by two sources, one "natural" and one "conventional." Both sources are available to the Egyptians; neither, the priest explained, are available to the Greeks. The natural source is the geography of the area and the floods and fires which periodically wreak great destruction upon the region, the cause of which is not the myth of Phaethon but the shifting of the heavenly bodies (according to the priest). The rising of the Nile saves the Egyptians from fire on the one hand and keeps them safe from floods on the other, whereas in Greece the learned people of the low-lying cities are wiped out by floods, leaving behind only the illiterate mountain-dwellers.

The conventional source of "transportation" is the art of writing, by virtue of which the Egyptians are able to preserve their history accurately. The Greeks, by contrast, must always begin anew after each scourge, since all the writers, who are city dwellers, have been wiped out by the floods. This is why the priest says "O Solon, Solon, you Greeks are always children, there is not such a thing as an old Greek." (22b4–5) The Greeks are always "young in soul" because they must, out of an illiterate and unmusical state, fashion accounts and poems—*myths*—anew each time. The older and wiser Egyptians, however, have no need of recourse to myths. They can provide the truth underlying both the myths and the myth-making impulse, since they have "the writing itself." (*auta ta grammata*)(24a1)

However, certain features of Critias' tale undermine what he purports to say. First of all, in his anti-mythical speech about Solon which has traversed several generations, Critias has clearly mythologized Solon, who (he proudly notes) was a friend of his great-grandfather. Solon was both the wisest man in all things and the noblest poet, so noble that if his wisdom and courage did not call him to other tasks he would surely have dwarfed Homer and Hesiod in fame. (21c4–d3) This is the stuff of the celebration of heroes in poetry, not of sober historiography. Old Athens is also mythologized, given form not by actual events but first of all by the goddess who gives it its name, "herself both a lover of war and a lover of wisdom." (24c8-d1) In Critias' account, the city develops and performs in accord with the mythical source of its origin. No real detail is given. Finally, the Atlantis tale is presented as a true account, but has all the signs of poetic tragedy. There is a hostile race governed by "kings of great and wondrous power" (25a6) on a faraway island. The Atlantans commit *hubris* and the city guided by Athena defeats them. Then both Athenians and Atlantans are swallowed up by the earth. The purported anti-mythical speech is riddled throughout by *mythos* in stock form.

This culminating and inadvertent declaration of the mythical origin of the Athens of which (according to Critias) Socrates (who named no city) spoke in the *Republic* affirms the presence of *mythos* in human *logos* generally and especially in the founding of republics (*politeiai*). The darkness which gave rise to the tale of Critias—the passage of time, the unreliability of oral reports both in general and as told by old men, the need for a great and mysterious origin, and the blindness to all of these—expose this abiding presence at the heart of *logos* in terms both of the tale and of the teller.

Both dialogues playfully treat *mythos* as if it could somehow be set at a distance, either mastered or dispensed with. In the *Republic*, this distancing of *mythos* results in the building of a city in speech which can exist only by some chance in the *future*,[93] or merely "in *logos*, since I don't suppose it exists anywhere on earth." (*Republic* 592a10–b1)[94] In the *Timaeus*, the distancing results in a tale of a similarly wondrous city as existing in the far-distant *past*, so long ago that there is no possibility of verification beyond the word of an old speaker whose credentials consist entirely of his having heard the tale from other old speakers. Concerning the actual city of the *present*, neither dialogue has much to say that is clear.

But this silence, or lack of clear insight, into the interplay of *mythos* and *logos* in the city of the present is no careless omission, nor does it bear witness to some serious defect in the present city. Rather, it testifies to the confusing intertwining of elements which occur in the fashioning of any city. Their co-presence testifies to the co-presence of the twin needs mentioned earlier, namely for a just and orderly city and for the nourishment of a whole human soul. Perhaps if *mythos* were not at the heart of both, these two needs might be harmonized. But this, of course, is another myth, issuing out of another region of our blindness. Whatever shape such a city—of the very distant past, or in the very distant future—might have, the *politeiai* of the present must cope with the troublesome mixture.

Thus once again, the tension in the city is reflected in the tension in *logos* between the two-fold myth-making function which gives rise to the dialogical anomalies concerning cities. The *Republic* and the *Timaeus*, in this regard, expose a certain playfulness in terms of time: the tension is relieved by either projecting the harmonized city so far forward into an indefinite future or so far back into an unknowable past that no inspection of it is possible. In this way, the darkness and ignorance at its core, which gives rise to the tension, can be concealed. But this playful projection, at the same time as it conceals the darkness and ignorance of its core, exposes the truth of the city of the present: that it is beset by ills of all kinds, that it lacks many of the qualities associated with the mythical cities, but that unlike its splendid counterparts, it is the real site of the human struggle. The city is the place where *philosophy* occurs.

In the projected aristocratic city of the *Republic*, there is no philosophy: guardians, auxiliaries and artisans comprise the entire population. And the noble city of the distant past presented in the *Timaeus* is presented as the actualization of this projected city: again, no philosophy takes place there. With all needs somehow answered, and with the central opinions accepted and fought for without question, and therefore with play excised, there is no place for the challenge of views and the often free-floating explorations of philosophy. Also, there is no place for this kind of myth-making in either of these mythically founded cities!

So the making of myths, itself a playful activity, has led to the expulsion of *mythos* from the cities in *logos*. On one level, this marks the cities in *logos* as non-human cities, which occur to the reader as distant and probably non-attainable. But on another level, these cities in *logos* are playthings: images through which the soul can vicariously experience some measure of truth about the human cities, and about its would-be "replacements." On the first level, the "ideality" of the non-human cities can be seen as providing a critique for what is missing in the actual cities of the present. On the second and deeper level, it can be seen as a celebration of the actual city and of the myth-making art which has grown in it.

In this regard, it would surely be appropriate to regard Platonic reflections on cities through their "ideal" counterparts as critical comments upon their shortcomings and/or as meaningful suggestions for reform.[95] More fundamentally, however, they are manifestations of the play of light and dark in the realm of human life in the city, and far from excising the darkness belong to this life in the so-called "ideal," they playfully expose it. The cities in *logos* flash this darkness out of every feature, most especially where they try to conceal it in the clear light of reason.

A word on the so-called ideality of cities, and on ideality as a whole, is in order. For the interpretation of the Platonic dialogues both on cities and in general, it is important to remember that "ideal" is not a Greek word, and that the notion of "ideal" as an individual incorporating all favorable properties and no unfavorable ones does not occur until many centuries later. Even the word *idea* in Greek, with its peculiarly Platonic sense as the correlate of a pure noetic seeing, preserves the sense of a thing's look.[96] While it is tempting to ascribe an ideal city to Plato (in the sense of a flawless city), this is a temptation that is indulged at one's philosophical peril. Vicarious images, and not distant hopes, are the material of the Platonic dialogues.

To conclude this chapter, it is preposterous to separate out two languages, one of *mythos* and one of *logos*, in the Platonic dialogues. (This is another reason why it goes against their main movement to speak of ideal cities as serious proposals of any kind.) These dialogues on cities have shown their essential intertwining. The two can be treated separately only in a rough fashion and only with many qualifications which account for the nature and degree of their separability. When they are treated as rigorously and seriously separated, the results are ridiculous (guardians carefully educated for injustice, an internally self-contradictory philosopher-king). But this indicates that in human speech, *mythos* and *logos* are at play, and are most at play when they are said not to be at play at all.

Myths are fashioned in actual cities, out of the needs and shortcomings of the citizens of these cities. Whether myths point backward to a great origin or forward to a great future, and whether their service is to cities or to the individual souls that dwell within them, the lack out of which they are born is apparent from their very telling. But their strength is also manifest, both in the power of their imagery to draw the soul forward to them and in the areas of questioning they open up. The gods and heroes of Homer's *Iliad* bear scant resemblance to the Greek citizens who employ them as images centuries after their creation (and to us),[97] but it is precisely their magnitude and their distance which allows their images to serve as measuring participants—vicarious images—in dialogues which seek to meet individual and political needs.

As the next chapter will show, Plato draws heavily upon Homeric imagery in the *Republic*, the *Ion*, and the *Lesser Hippias*, engaging it at close quarters in the course of the philosophical questioning it inspires. In the first case, the image of Achilles in Hades serves as a focal point whereby the role of vicarious imagery in cities can be distinguished from its sharply different role for individuals. The treatment of the *Ion* distances the imagery from the human beings who create, disseminate and enjoy it in terms of origin—and from their cities as well. The treatment of the *Lesser Hippias* assigns a power to that imagery which overtakes even its employers. But as we shall see, neither this imagery nor that questioning can dispense with one another. Each is bound to the other in the play of the Platonic dialogues.

CHAPTER SEVEN:
PHILOSOPHY AND POETRY IN THE CITY I
(HOMER AND THE TRAGIC POETS)

Contrary to the received wisdom on Plato, Homer and the tragic poets[98] (a wisdom which, happily, is receding more and more[99]), the Platonic dialogues do not advocate censorship, nor are they "against" poetry. It is one part of the purpose of this chapter to put this issue finally and decisively to rest, and another to show how thoroughly and how positively poetry and philosophy nourish and belong to one another in Plato, despite the dangers.

The philosopher as thoughtful interpreter is the voice of the *Republic,* and not some poetry-censoring would-be tyrant. The kinship and the conflict of poetry and philosophy in Plato's *Republic* cannot be properly appraised unless the manner in which these two ways of *logos* perform the same function is understood. Both address the individual human soul in the deepest way, attending to its most fundamental concerns and touching it where it is both most vulnerable and most hopeful: its pleasure and pain, its knowledge and ignorance, and its goodness and badness. In so doing, both poetry and philosophy contest the claims, which are just claims, of the actual city.

This contest, which serves as a meeting place for some of the weightiest issues confronting the human soul, is profoundly playful because of the high stakes, not in spite of them. The human soul orients itself and addresses its challenges (1) in terms of the ideas which it thinks and speaks of, and (2) in terms of the images which animate and direct it. The two correspond, but only roughly as we have seen, to the callings of philosophy and poetry. Philosophy is born from wonder, poetry from inspiration. While there is much crossing, the former occupies itself primarily with thought and its limits, the latter with the creation of beautiful images. Political life provides a principal occasion for both, since both the philosopher and the poet find themselves in the city amidst much thought, much speech, and much pursuit of perceived beauty at play in and around them.

As members of a city, both poets and philosophers are engaged in political life by necessity. The obligations of citizenship must be regarded as serious; there is no room to dismiss or to mitigate them.[100] Mere voluntary presence in the city binds the citizen to its laws and practices. (cf. *Crito* 51c6–52a5) But in light of the capacity of the soul to question and to create from the material available through political life, a space opens up for the soul in which it might fashion another sort of home. The soul can play in this space, seeking and trying out thoughts and images in order to find what is most suitable. In this way, poets and philosophers disengage from the political life in which they find themselves situated.

This playful disengagement from the realm of the actual city takes place as an engagement with philosophy and/or with poetry. This is the threat to the actual city, that this playful disengagement might provoke a serious one. This first section of this chapter will treat this threat and its resolution as it occurs in the *Republic*. The second will treat the philosophy/poetry relation in terms of their sources in relation both to the city and to the soul by means of an interpretation of the *Ion*, which will secure the place of Homeric poetry in the soul's quest for what is best. The third will exhibit the subtle, powerful interplay of the Homeric heroes within Socratic questioning in the *Lesser Hippias*, demonstrating an interrelation of vicarious imagery and philosophy.

* *

The objection is raised by Socrates in the second and third books of the *Republic* against permitting certain kinds of poetry in the purged city (the one in which the phantom of justice is sighted) precisely because such poetry threatens the stability of the bonds of absolute identification of human being and city, a stability which the guardians must maintain in order to be true guardians. More precisely, certain poetry threatens the preservation of the opinion of what is terrible, a preservation which is central to the guardians' bearing. (429b8–d1) That is, by presenting heroes as fearful of death, or by singing of the gods as acting against their ruler Zeus, certain poetical passages and rhythms disrupt the bond of guardian and city, provoke the guardians to call the prevailing opinion into question, and thereby introduce distrust of this opinion into the soul of the guardian. This distrust endangers the city, as certain shared opinions form the basis of its existence and preservation.

But philosophy introduces the same distrust. Namely, philosophy provokes the one in whose soul it has taken hold to call prevailing opinions, indeed all opinions, into question. In so doing, it introduces doubt in the soul where previously there was assurance. This likeness of function, namely of challenging the bond of opinion and in so doing of breaking the bond of complete identification of human being and city, constitutes the core of both the kinship and the quarrel. Bonds of human being with convention and of human being with prevailing political orthodoxy are disrupted with this challenge. In both the experience of poetry and the experience of philosophy, the city is, in a way, left behind by the soul. This is so whether the destination be the lower reaches of Hades or the upper reaches of the back of the heavens (*epi to tou ouranou nōtō*). (*Phaedrus*, 247b7–c1) The kinship concerns this common deed, the quarrel concerns the way the deed occurs, i.e. the direction which is both taken and prescribed in the performance of the deed. In other words, the quarrel concerns the measure of the deed. So poetry measures philosophy and finds it empty. Philosophy measures poetry and finds it ignorant. (*Republic* 607b1–c2) Philosophy lacks beautiful images; poetry lacks critical accounts.

The quarrel and kinship (and these are not ultimately separable) can be seen clearly in the contrast between the two contexts within the *Republic* in which the "Achilles in Hades" passage from Book XI of the *Odyssey* appears:

> I would rather be on the soil, a serf to another, to a man without lot whose means
> of life are not great, than rule over all of the dead who have perished. (*Republic*
> 386c5–70; *Odyssey*, XI, 489–491).

The passage first appears at the beginning of Book III, where Socrates seems to profess the most unambiguous disapproval. He is concerned that hearing Homer's words would introduce a dangerous fear of death into the souls of the guardians. In fact, it is the first such passage he would ban from his city. (386c4)

Its next appearance is shortly after Book VII opens, and occurs after the human being who has been liberated from the cave has had a taste of life on the earth. Socrates notes that such a man would have no desire for the honors bestowed by the men who live among the shadows, and would rather " 'be on the soil, a serf to another man, to a portionless man' than to opine those things and live that way." (516d5–7)

Several matters should be noted about this apparent reversal of sentiment:

1) Only when considered from the standpoint of the total identification of human being and city does the passage in question become dangerous, for in this context the hero is interpreted straightforwardly as one who should in all aspects be imitated. When freed from the bond to the city (when freed from the bond to convention and to opinion), another possibility of interpreting the hero arises: no longer is the hero a kind of "original" to be imitated, but rather the hero functions as a vicarious image of a human life properly lived. In this context, the words of Achilles are heard to say not that death is fearful and that even the most sniveling life on earth is preferable. Rather, they are interpreted to say that to live among shadows without being, i.e. to live holding blind opinions—even to be named king in the realm where blind opinions are honored—is worth nothing to the one who has come to see more clearly. Anything, even the greatest suffering or the

greatest dishonor, is preferable to such a life.

2) Since the Homeric passage is the same one cited in Book III and Book VII, the crucial factor cannot be the poetical passage. The framework of its interpretation, and not the image created by the poet, is the issue. Poetry does not come complete with its own interpretation, and every interpretation of poetry occurs within a certain framework; we have considered two divergent ones. At the least, this says that poetry by itself is not a culprit. Any harm it may do, as we indicated earlier, does not belong to its nature, but occurs as a result of where and how it is employed. It cannot be held accountable for being interpreted in certain, perhaps subversive, ways.

3) Only the one who has been liberated from the cave, who has been liberated in some way from the condition (*pathei*) of the city and its education, i.e. only the one who has seen the shadows as shadows and knows that they are not real being, is able to hear the poem in a thoughtful way. To such a one, the poem images his condition as a human being seeking a life governed by love of truth, as opposed to one in which political opinions are accepted without serious question. This says: only someone in whom *philosophy* has begun to take hold (for the task of seeing opinions as opinions, i.e. of recognizing one's own ignorance and the partiality of one's insight, is among philosophy's most basic tasks) can interpret the poem in a healthy manner, one which does not subvert the proper humanity of the soul. In this sense, philosophy is required in order for poetry to be properly heard. So poetry needs philosophy as its measure, not of the poetic art itself but as work to be received appropriately by human beings.

4) Only the one who has made the ascent out of the cave, whose soul has been "turned around (*periagōgēs*)" (518d4), can develop such an interpretation out of his or her own resources. The poem does not teach anything, but merely shows what lies already within, perhaps making the soul's powers manifest for the first time. In the case of the guardian who is to identify totally with the city, only poetry which would inculcate the desired opinion of what is terrible and what is honorable is permitted. Therefore the heroes and the gods must conform to specifications of the founders, for the liberation which would permit a healthy interpretation of

this passage would risk the death of the city; but this liberation is precisely what the founders of this unjust city must avoid and banish from their city.[101]

With these considerations in mind, much of Book X is recast. Although the book begins with a recollection of the reflections on poetry of Books II and III, which Socrates deems as "particularly right" (595a2—*mallon orthōs*) with respect to the founding of "this" city, it is hardly unequivocal which city he refers to, as we have already seen in another context[102]. If the reference is taken as specific, "this city" may refer to the republic (*politeia*) of the soul with which Book IX concludes, or to the aristocratic city with which Book IV concludes and from which Book VIII proceeds, or to the city in *logos* which can cut across all cities, or even to the actual cities. For although Socrates begins by speaking of the "maiming of thought" (595b5–6) produced by imitative poetry, suggesting that the individual soul apart from the city is his concern, he speaks throughout his harshest passage (605a6–c3) primarily in terms of the pernicious influence it exercises upon the people of the city, and mentions the corrupting of the private man only as an afterthought.

Several other peculiarities make clear that Socrates' remarks cannot be taken as straightforward condemnation. For example:

a) If the imitative part of poetry "maims the thought (*dianoia*) of those who hear them. . .," then Socrates too, who is impressively conversant with the body of tragedy and of poetry in general, has been maimed.[103] But the *logos* continues: ". . . and do not have knowledge of how they really are (*to eidenai auta hoia tugchanei onta*), [which would serve] as a remedy (*pharmakon*)." (595b3–7) Socrates' knowledge, then, serves as a countercharm, which implies that the poems do not by their nature maim thought, but maim only the thought of those who do not know the real being of such poetry. Knowledge of the real being of this poetry serves as a *pharmakon*, which can be translated straightforwardly as a medicine or remedy, but also as a drug, potion, charm, spell, enchantment.[104] In any case (and the "cases" will be explored further in Chapter 9 on the *pharmakon* of writing and Chapter 11 on imitation), a transformation of one's state by non-rational means, in this case the *pharmakon* of knowledge, heals the maiming of thought (*dianoia*) by imitative poetry.

But this says: thought (*dianoia*), an affection (*pathē*) of the soul on the intelligible side of the divided line, can be harmed (perhaps grievously) by a provocation from the side of the sensible. It also says that knowledge of real being, which belongs on the intelligible side of the line, provides non-rational restoration to this sense-distorted thought. No account is given of how the line between intelligible and sensible can be breached in these dramatic ways.

In a way, the two interpretations of the "Achilles in Hades" passage exemplify unhealthy and healthy approaches to poetry. The first would promote fear of death and preference for even the basest life. The second would promote fear of a false life and celebration of a true one. Both show the influence of a powerful image upon the soul of its hearer. The difference is the contact of the second interpreter with the world that shapes the opinions (shadows), a contact which provokes awareness of his own reflective capacities (i.e. with the top portion of the divided line).

But none of this establishes the inherent danger of poetry, or its actual danger to anyone. The orientation of thought to images is the abiding and decisive countertheme to the separation of sensible and intelligible. A direct and serious condemnation of poetry also condemns this unavoidable and essential orientation of the human soul. Thus, the apparent denigration of poetry in Book X must be understood together with its celebration: whatever danger it may present to the human soul, poetry is shown to be a source of nourishment as well. This danger and that nourishment both belong to the play of the Platonic dialogues. Thus, to maintain that Plato condemns poetry as a philosophical position is one-sided, and neglects the more originary play to which this condemnation belongs.

b) The condemnation of Homer is also hardly straightforward.[105] The charges of ignorance, and of his inability to found a school or an enduring tradition of disciples which would make men better, are unconvincing because—as Socrates knows—the same charges could be levelled against *him*, if indeed they are charges. That they are not serious charges is clearly indicated by Socrates' selection of certain sophists (600c1–d4) as examples of men who, unlike Homer, know how to make citizens better and who have built an enduring following. In distinguishing Homer so clearly from the same sophists from whom he also distinguishes himself, his positive kinship with Homer is subtly affirmed. So, then, is the positive kinship of philosophy and poetry.

c) Socrates remarks that only poetry which celebrates gods and heroes and good men in songs of praise should be admitted into the city. (607a3–8) But this proscription excludes no poetry at all by Homer and the tragedians.

So the playfulness of the contest with Homer is clear and incontrovertible, once this contest is framed in the proper way. In a sense, the playfulness can be seen as the play of tragedy, since it is the inevitable human shattering against death which gives rise to the issues treated by philosophy and poetry, and which animates certain key images of the hero (Achilles) and the philosopher (Socrates). But they are also vicarious images in kinship with one another, and can be seen in this light as images capable of turning a human being away from one kind of life (dominated by shadows, opinions) toward another, worthier one for a human being, if they are received appropriately.

As we have seen, there is no way to receive the *Republic* as a diatribe against poetry and do justice to the whole of its *logos*. The inspired images of poetry, together with the thoughtful ones of philosophy, require a different sort of reception. The images assert no doctrines and take no positions, but playfully elicit in the soul a proper regard for what concerns it most of all.

* *

Ion's political identity is ambiguous. He is an Ephesian, and Ephesus is under the military governance of Athens. He affirms his identity as an Athenian rhapsode at 530b1, where he refers to the Athenian rhapsodes as "we" (*ēnengkametha*) who won first prize. At 541c3 he and Socrates discuss generalship, where it first appears that Ion's political origin precludes his being named a general. But Socrates names several aliens who attained generalships. Thus, one's skill (*technē*) or one's gift can and does enable one to transcend political origin. And political identity itself is, in fact, somewhat fluid rather than simply given as fixed.

The rhapsode takes his art from place to place: perhaps to Ephesus, perhaps to Epidaurus, perhaps to the various cities represented at the Panathenaea. (530a1–b3) Ion is celebrated as the rhapsode who best brings the music of Homer to his hearers. But he does not know the meaning of what he sings, as Socrates' questioning discloses. The principal point is not Ion's obtuseness. It is that the work of the god can get done without any knowledge either on the part of the rhapsode or of the audience. The accomplishment of the god's work is imaged by the stone of Herakleia, which binds the god to the people in a chain whose rings consist of the Muse, the inspired poet, and (it turns out) the rhapsode. (533c9–535a1) Absent are good sense (*emphrones*), intellect (*nous*) and skill (*technē*). Present are inspiration (*entheōs*), possession (*embōsin*), divine power (*theia dunamei*). The blindness and senselessness of the poet has the function of introducing measure into the Bacchic transport inspired by the poem. The infirmity of the poet reminds that it is the god and not the human being who is the source of the poem, i.e. that human insight had nothing to do with the creation of the poem in its beauty. (534c7–d4) And the mere rhapsode is further removed from the divine source than the inspired poet.

Even the blind, uncomprehending chanting of the rhapsode makes possible the movement of the human soul away from the common involvement in sensation (*aisthēsis*) and opinion which reinforces the fear-begetting bond to the body. By non-rational means (the gifts of the poet and the rhapsode) and through the *aisthēsis* peculiar to art inspired by the Muses, the poetry of Homer transports the hearer to a place in the soul where the transformation of this bond into a bond of another kind becomes possible. The vicarious undergoing of the tragic things can turn the soul toward more fundamental human concerns, encouraging it to be more confident in the face of difficulties, and more thoughtful toward its life.

The poetry of Homer is political in the sense that the *polis* is the site of its performance, and it is trans-local in that the citizens of many different cities (which share a common language) can hear it. It is part of its cities. There is no doubt in the dialogues, however, that the stretch of the political—however fluid it may be—is not complete. To be a citizen of Athens, for example, means that there is a realm where the political power of Athens cannot reach; there is a realm that is one's own (*idia*) and another that is public (*demousia*) (*Apology* 30b4) In the *Apology* (which will occupy much of the next chapter), Socrates cites several non-rational sources beyond the city for the behavior which has brought him before the tribunal of the city: the god (30a5–7) who commanded his service to the city of challenging his fellow citizens to care for their souls, his *daimonion* (31d1) which opposes his engagement in politics, and once again *Homer* (28b2–d5), whose poetry provides powerful images of worthy conduct in the face of death.

These non-rational sources are accompanied by the well-known *logoi* which argue them rationally, but neither way of addressing these crucial issues can be said to have clear preference. There is no epistemological certainty. There is no authoritatively direct non-rational disclosure. But to say that this leads either to a kind of relativism or pragmatism in Plato is mistaken: the play of the poetical and the philosophical provides its own measure. To be cheerless or resigned or pessimistic, or even confidently doctrinal, is ruled out. The power of questioning and the stone of Herakleia, these playthings, comprise the "rules" of the game.

* *

If we alter our view of the *Lesser Hippias* and look at it primarily as an encounter of human beings with Homeric heroes and not so much as another philosophy/sophistry encounter, we can see a bit further how poetical images and philosophical thought are at play with one another and how their mutual interpenetration clears a proper region for the soul.

The dialogue begins with a silence, the silence of Socrates after hearing Hippias' discourse upon Homer, and its turning point is another silence threatened by Hippias after Socrates' *elenchos* of the former's willing/unwilling (*akonti/hekonti*) distinction. (371e9–372d1) Both are mediated by Eudikos, and this mediation of the silences is his sole and crucial function.[106] Hippias is presented as the one who knows and can do all things, a caricature of a sophist. Socrates is presented as the most ignorant of all (and unable even to distinguish goodness from power), a caricature of himself as philosopher.

By contrast, Homer's heroes Achilles and Odysseus, who can be seen as poetic enlargements (and in that sense, caricatures) of men, appear in their full humanity. Both Achilles and Odysseus are shown to tell the truth at some times and to lie at others, yet their stature never suffers: Socrates and Hippias regard them both as excellent men, although from different sides.

Hippias' speech (not itself presented) treats the famous embassy of Odysseus, Aias and Peleus to Achilles in Book IX of the *Iliad*. Hippias argues that Achilles is superior to Odysseus as a "kind of man" because the former is true (*alēthēs*) and simple (*haplous*) while the latter is "many-wayed" (*polutropos*) and false (*pseudēs*). (365b3–5) Socrates, citing Achilles' many conflicting accounts of his plans and Odysseus' simple trust of the account given to him by Achilles, argues instead for Odysseus' honesty and Achilles' guile. Hippias then maintains that Achilles lies unwillingly while the lies of Odysseus are willing. But Socrates leads him to agree that the one who acts willingly is always better than the unwilling. For example, the runner who can run both rapidly and slowly is better than the one who has no choice but to run slowly (373c1–374a1). The reasoning is similar for other arts, for sciences, and ultimately for justice. Surprisingly and preposterously, this line of reasoning leads to the conclusion that the man who voluntarily does disgraceful (*aischra*) and unjust things is good.

This ending is unsatisfactory to both Hippias and Socrates, and one is tempted to call it aporetic. Socrates, assuming the role of the perplexed innocent, chides the "wise" Hippias for not giving him guidance. We are brought before our ignorance, are called to begin again, and are presumably in better condition to philosophize by virtue of the exercise. There is no denying this. But things look somewhat different from the point of view of the playful inversion, according to which the interlocutors are caricatured in the dialogue and the heroes are reduced to ordinary mortals.

Retracing the path to the aporetic ending in terms of the role of poetic imagery in the *Lesser Hippias*, Socrates presumably leaves Homer behind near the beginning of the inquiry "since we are incapable of asking him his thoughts (*noon*) on the verses he has made." (365c9–d1) Near the end, he says that his perplexity—confirmed by the bad result of the inquiry—causes Socrates, causes other ordinary people like him, and causes even the "wise" sophists like Hippias *to wander*. (*planasthai*[107] 367c3) The word "wander" is used four times in the last four lines, and is the last word in the dialogue. In terms of the poetic elements of the dialogue, *Odysseus* is the famous wanderer in Homeric poetry.

In the *Odyssey*, Odysseus reclaims his home in the guise of an ordinary beggar after wandering in search of great fame (*mega kleos*) for twenty years. In the myth which concludes another dialogue, Plato's *Republic*, Odysseus the wanderer is said to have been purified of love of honor and seeks the life of a private man who minds his own business. (620c1–d3) In this way, muddling about honestly in mere confusion on the level of argument is presented as a heroic journey home on the level of poetic imagery.

So Homer's poetry, said earlier to be left behind, playfully returns and frames the discourse, which at its conclusion is shadowed by the image of wandering Odysseus.[108] At the close of the *Lesser Hippias*, the poetic travels of Odysseus intertwine with the philosophical forays of Socrates, and are joined in the image of wandering to which the falsely confident Hippias has been playfully invited. Taken together with the role of Achilles in the ascent out of the cave, the great Homeric heroes belong to philosophy as vicarious images of fearlessness toward truth and toward disdaining unexamined opinion (shadows), and willingness to wander in confusion rather than profess something unworthy until a way (home) to wisdom is found. In this way, the dialogues weave the inspired poetry of Homer and the thoughtful questioning of Socrates such that neither determines the other, leaving both at play.

CHAPTER EIGHT:
PHILOSOPHY AND POETRY IN THE CITY II
(COMEDY: ARISTOPHANES AND
THE APOLOGY)

Socrates proclaimed a hunger for images at *Republic* 487e4–488a2,[109] but declared no such hunger in his defense as presented in the *Apology*. The image he craves least of all is the one of himself fashioned by the only one of his old accusers whose name he knows, and "who happens to be a certain comic poet." (18d1–2) In his defense before his fellow Athenians, Socrates seems to expel the playfulness that characterizes his activity in other contexts: "perhaps it will seem to some of you that I am playing, but be assured that I will tell you the whole truth." (20d4–6) But the deeper movement of the dialogue reasserts this play.

The mutual nourishing and belonging together of philosophy and poetry, discussed in the previous chapter, receives its greatest challenge in the life of Socrates from the images of *comedy*, not in the confrontation of philosophy with Homer and tragedy. The previous chapter established the complementarity of philosophy and Homeric poetry in the *Republic*. It is also present in the *Apology*, where Socrates employs Homeric images in his defense.[110] But no such employment is possible in the case of Aristophanic imagery. Nevertheless, the battle of Socrates to overcome his comic caricature by Aristophanes in *Clouds* serves as a mask for the deep bond also shared by philosophy and comedy.

On one level, the poetic gift of Aristophanes gives the stock charges against the philosopher a vividness and a comic richness which would make them all the more difficult to shake: a lizard defecates into the open mouth of a heavenward-gazing Socrates[111]; the philosopher's disciples bend over the more closely to survey with their eyes what is beneath the ground, as their rumps are aimed at the heavens which would so pointedly mark their master[112]; weaker *logos* defeats stronger *logos* largely through recourse to buggery.[113]

In the *Apology*, Socrates notes the great difficulty he will have in fighting shadows (*skiamachein*). What shadows these are! He complains that there is no cross-examination possible with no one to cross-examine. On the one hand there is the clear and obvious reason for this impossibility: the prejudices begotten through such powerful imagery are too deeply rooted to excise, and its originator(s) are long gone and probably forgotten. But the more subtle reason in the case of Aristophanes, as in the case of Homer, is the paradox in the comportment of the philosopher toward images, which consists of an ever-present need for them and an equally present need to transcend them. This paradox is experienced most sharply when great artists like Homer and Aristophanes are their inspired makers.

The pointedness of this case arises from the fact that the principal shadow with which Socrates must contend is no mere general accusation about philosophers whispered out of his earshot to innocent ears, but a powerfully specific and vivid image of Socrates himself created by precisely such an artist, and presented to his fellow citizens at the Dionysian festival in 399 B.C.. Against this image and its impact (as well as against the more general and ethereal shadows), Socrates will try to present the truth about himself in 423 B.C. to the judges he will not call true judges, but merely "men of Athens." (17a1)

But it quickly becomes clear that it is not so much a contest between the true Socrates and his image as it is a contest between *two images* of Socrates, with his provocative words and deeds in the *Apology* fashioning the competing image. Despite his apparent insistence upon presenting the true Socrates in opposition to a comic image of him, it should hardly be any surprise that Socrates is engaged with images in the *Apology*: he is always engaged with them, even as he endeavors at times to transcend them. The special circumstance here is that he must contend with *his own* image. The nature of this contest shapes the self-image he presents.

Next to the babbler and evasive fraud of *Clouds*, the *Apology* juxtaposes an aggressive, direct attacker who instructs his judges on the meaning of their oath (18a2–6), who likens his behavior in Athens to that of Achilles in Troy (28b9–28d5), and who proposes a reward for himself rather than a penalty upon his conviction. (36d1–d9) Just as no one had ever encountered a Socrates resembling the one seen in *Clouds*, no Socratic behavior which approaches such continuous stridency and anger occurs anywhere else in the Platonic corpus. To maintain that both images are poetic in the same sense would be excessive. But it seems clear, in light of the early and pointed reference to Aristophanes, that the Aristophanic Socrates in *Clouds* called forth the Platonic Socrates of the *Apology*.

So a comic image has called forth a philosophical image; philosophy is in some way appropriated to comedy in the Platonic dialogues. In a straightforward sense, it appears that the distortions of comic poetry call forth the measure-providing corrective *logos* of philosophy as *pharmakon,* just as in the case of Homer and the tragedians.[114] But as we have seen, the image of Socrates in the *Apology* is unusual in its stridency and humorlessness. This stridency and absence of play cannot explained by the seriousness of the trial: in the *Phaedo*, in the face of death, Socrates exudes playfulness and good cheer.

This inner relation of comedy and philosophy is the crucial issue in the effort to understand the strange image of Socrates and his uncharacteristically serious tone in the *Apology*, quite apart from the issues which tend to dominate the scholarship.[115] Whatever the conscious purposes of Aristophanes and whatever the actual historical and cultural circumstances might have been, the battle in Plato's *Apology* over the image of Socrates does not have much to do with the intentions and larger purpose of individual actors on certain stages—not, at least, in terms of its philosophical significance. At issue is the ancient quarrel, which we treated with respect to tragedy in the previous chapter.[116] Here the quarrel occurs with respect to comedy, which results in a different but kindred reconciliation.

There is no doubt that although the Aristophanic image (or at least what it represents to Socrates as the source of the old accusations) proved too powerful to overcome at the actual trial, the philosophical image of Socrates presented by Plato has triumphed since. While the old accusations against philosophers still surface and thus are, in a sense, still influential, the defense of Socrates as a defense of philosophy and philosophers who are worthy of the name is widely if not near universally regarded as entirely successful. It is obvious that the Socratic image in the *Apology* is closer to an accurate representation of philosophical activity than the image of the sophistical natterer in *Clouds*, even if the most generous allowance is made and if Aristophanes' intention is interpreted as entirely friendly. Nevertheless, the image of Socrates in the *Apology* is distorted as well as incomplete, and in important ways, inaccurate.

Perhaps surprisingly, the most likely candidate for an appropriate complement to the partial image in the *Apology* is that same image in *Clouds* with which Socrates must fight for his life and which he would expel from the atmosphere of his trial. The fight on the level of history, with this image powerfully in the background, resulted in the successful prosecution by Meletus and Anytus of Socrates which led to his death. However, on the level of the ancient quarrel, the serious and sober image of Socrates rejoins with its playful and liberated counterpart. On the former level, the images of honorable and serious servant and subversive and frivolous fraud opposed one another; there could be no compromise. On the latter level, a seriousness which excluded all play (Socrates of *Apology*) opposed a playfulness which excluded all seriousness (Socrates of *Clouds*). On this level, the two partial images merge, and the Socrates of the other dialogues who both argues and plays is genuinely re-encountered. The comic image provided by

Aristophanes in *Clouds* fills out the serious one presented in Plato's *Apology*. In another formulation, the opposition which occurs as serious on the level of history and which led to the conviction of Socrates[117] occurs as play on the level of the quarrel between philosophy and poetry.

The attempted expulsion of playfulness can be attributed to Socrates' need to suppress both the poetic in general and the Aristophanic-comic in particular in order to present his defense to the "men of Athens," a defense which is commanded by the obligations of citizenship. He will "tell the truth" which is his obligation in his position as speaker (*rhētoros*)(18a5–6), and in so doing attempt to answer the charges of the comic poet *as if they were not playful but only serious*. The charges are treated as detached from their specific location in the poem of *Clouds* and in the sacred setting of the Dionysian festival: they are treated as if they were actual accusations. In defending himself against the charges of professing arcane knowledge and making the weaker argument appear stronger, Socrates finds himself defending philosophy "against" poetry in the setting of the city at its most "political." The poets "say things many and beautiful, but know none of the things they say," (22c3–4) although they thought they were wise. They lack the recognition of ignorance necessary for genuine philosophical activity and even for gaining knowledge generally. They proceeded "by nature and inspiration, like prophets and the givers of oracles." (22c1–2) Their difference presents itself sharply: to travel the path of the philosopher requires great seriousness, involving perpetual self-reflection and self-criticism. The path of the poet, even of the tragic poet, seems more playful and innocent, involving the mere discharge of one's nature and/or gift.

The Socrates of other dialogues does not so radically oppose the poetical, as we have seen. Recourses to non-rational sources abound. To cite just a few cases, he allows the authority of dreams in the *Phaedo* to lead him to practice music on his final day. (60e4–8) In the *Symposium*, he strongly implies that the poets beget the worthiest children of all. (209c9–d4) In the *Apology*, he is instructed not only by his divine sign (40b1—*tou theos sēmion*), but also by "oracles and dreams and every way." (33c5–6) Even in the *Meno*, where center stage seems to be held entirely by Socratic *elenchos*, he invokes the authority of certain priests and priestesses (81a5–c4) and declares the source of virtue as divine dispensation in his final hypothesis. (99e6) And the *Republic* calls for poetry, with its non-rational origin, to give an account of itself in order to be admitted to the city, while arguments (*logoi*) are to be chanted.[118]

This call, which would bring together rational and non-rational sources, has already been answered both in poetry and in the dialogues. The "*Mēnin aeide, thea, Pēlēiadeō Achilēos*" ("Sing, goddess, the rage of Peleus' son, Achilles") of Homer's *Iliad* (I, l. 1) and the "*Mousasōn Helikōniadōn archōmeth' aeidein*" ("From the Helikonian Muses begin to sing") of Hesiod's *Theogony* (l. 1), and even the "*iou, iou: ō Zeu basileu*" ("Oh oh king Zeus") which opens *Clouds* may be seen as providing apologies in meter. In so doing, they wholly satisfy the requirements for admission to the city. While they are surely terse when compared with their philosophical counterparts, they acknowledge the inspiration spoken of Socrates in the *Apology* and with it the non-rational origin of their work. In this way, their measure is enacted in the poem itself.

From the side of philosophy, the Platonic dialogues themselves may be seen as chanted *logoi* on account of their playfulness and their often inspired speech. In this sense, they are instances of a certain music which charmingly fends off the charm of the beautiful images of the poets, which would otherwise overcome the reasoning powers of their entranced hearers. Measured by philosophical *logos*, these beautiful images serve as occasions for reflection upon and celebration of the most basic matters confronting human life (including the issue of how to deal with beautiful images!). By Homeric or Hesiodic standards the dialogues are musically moribund, but they are rich with myths, jests, sudden twists, and in general the drama and playfulness one finds in the poetry Socrates putatively criticizes. This odd complementarity, united by the common bond of philosophy and poetry to imagery, provides the condition for the surprising view that only when the Aristophanic image of Socrates in *Clouds* is added to the Platonic image in the *Apology* do we arrive at a just image of Socrates.

* *

The interpretation of the *Apology's* role in fashioning the image of Socrates shows perhaps more clearly than anywhere else the enormous distance between an Anglo-American approach to Plato such as that of Gregory Vlastos and his students, and an approach like that of Sallis and the one taken here. In looking at the *Apology*, Vlastos found in Socrates "a man who is all paradox."[119] He located as the central paradox the tension between Socrates' teaching of the salvation of the soul through knowledge on the one hand, and on the other his frequent proclamations of fundamental ignorance and his tireless destructive criticism of those who would profess a knowledge they did not possess. This is an accurate reading of the Socrates of the *Apology*. But it not only misses the Socrates of the other dialogues, it misses an even more fundamental paradox of Socrates, namely the paradox in which seriousness and playfulness are juxtaposed and intertwined.

In arguing for and celebrating Socrates' greatness, Vlastos lists his character, his moral influence, and above all his method. But the playfulness at the heart of Socrates' activity—so clearly present in his frequent unbalancing of conversations by means of a provocative interpolation, in his jests at the expense of/in delight in his remarkable appearance, in his voluminous and accurate knowledge of the poetry and mythology he declares is unnecessary and perhaps injurious to souls, and in his efforts to calm the fears of his friends on the day he is to die—is nowhere on his list. Perhaps these are absent in Vlastos' account because they are not prominent in the *Apology*, although an adequate characterization of Socrates in the Platonic dialogues should not be restricted to this one dialogue—especially not *this* one.

Vlastos' well-structured but tone-deaf essay maintains that (1) Socrates' character transformed his natural defects into virtues, (2) his moral nature reformed the human conscience and made it (rather than social class) the determinant of worth, and (3) his method made the aforementioned excellences open to every human being.[120] He adds that "a poet like Aristophanes sensed this without really understanding it."[121] Whether Aristophanes "really understood" Socrates' moral reformation or not, and whatever his real intention in *Clouds*, Aristophanes surely had an ear for one-sided sanctimoniousness, for a seriousness which would forget the comedy lurking in all things. (It is not often enough noted that the fruits of old education, which Aristophanes supposedly champions in *Clouds*, are also ridiculed: *"pugēn megalēn, posthēn mikran."*)[122]

Following the above outline but using *Clouds* and not the *Apology*, (1) Socrates' character is one which transforms whatever virtues are present in himself as well as in his disciples into defects, and magnifies already existing vices; (2) his moral reform consisted primarily of sophistry in service to swindling; and (3) his method consisted of preposterous enlargement and obfuscation of meaningless issues. These three are not merely casual pieces of ridicule designed to exploit a relatively easy target, whether with good will or with malice. These three features of the comic image represent excesses which are built into the philosophical character as perpetual possibilities, and against which this character must guard. That is, when one who would philosophize loses his/her sense of measure, the Aristophanic caricature ensues. One such loss arises when one forgets the ignorance to which one is given over, the awareness of which Socrates calls his "certain wisdom" (20d7–8) in the *Apology*. Another results from a seriousness that would exclude playfulness: in the *Republic* we hear Socrates say ". . . nor are any of the human things worthy of great seriousness." (604b12–c1)

This includes the practice of philosophy, to which an element of play must belong if it is to be worthy of its name. The serious prose of the *Apology* ironically requires the comic poetry of Aristophanes, against which it was first called to fight, in order to allow the truly philosophical image of Socrates to shine forth from it. In the context of the trial and the defense Socrates felt compelled to conduct (his *daimonion* never urges him to stop this defense), the playful is present as expelled and Aristophanes is treated as political accuser rather than as inspired poet. Bereft of the comic dimension, Socrates appears to be a besieged political martyr, an image which also occurs nowhere else in Plato.

And what about the true Socrates, the image which does justice to his nature? As we have seen, Socrates' nature is given over in fundamental ways to images, and the discussion of the sun, divided line and cave in Chapters 2 and 3 established that the bond of human beings in general to images is a fundamental and inalienable one. The two key poles of his philosophical activity, his recognition of ignorance and his thought of the forms (*eidē*), involve this bond. His playful comportment is a function of this peculiar bond. In the *Crito*, where Socrates is no longer compelled to speak in a *polis*-determined framework, we have seen how cavalierly he treats many politically valuable things: he places them in the same category as images used to manipulate and frighten young children.[123]

Socratic playfulness in the *Apology* cannot be suppressed entirely, and surfaces at the conclusion of his defense, where he issues a remarkable command to his supporters: when facing death, it is necessary (*chrē*) to be cheerful, to be of good hope (*euelpidas*). (41c8) Twinned with this command is another: to think (*dianoeisthai*) this one saying as truth, that to a good man no harm (*kakon*) can come either in life nor after. (41c8–d1) The former command assumes that the realm of feeling (*aisthēsis*) can be ruled by an act of thought. The latter command assumes that we have knowledge of an afterlife. The twin commands concluding this philosophical dialogue are playful: they treat humans as if they could leave behind the conditions of embodiment and of political life, i.e. as if they could live by pure thought[124]—just as Aristophanes created a Socrates in *Clouds* suitable for a purely poetic comedy.

This playfulness, which comically exaggerates the limits of human knowledge and human control over feeling, discloses a possibility left open at the heart of human thought and feeling in so doing. Socrates showed the more serious side of this playfulness at 29a4–b9, where he argued that to fear death is to fear what is not known, and is therefore disgraceful; injustice is to be feared, because the disgracefulness of doing injustice is known. The philosophical courage spoken of is possible even in the face of ignorance of an afterlife and of a human thought which is bound to sensation in inextricable ways. Nothing about human limits rule this courage out. Rather, this ignorance and this bond to sensation are conditions for its poetic and philosophical possibility as a response to the challenge these limits present.

* *

The comedy of the city in Book V of the *Republic* offers kindred playfulness and kindred possibility. It has been likened by some[125] to Aristophanes' *Ecclesiazousai* (*The Assembly of Women*), who see it as a contest with Aristophanes. While the parallels to the role of women in *Ecclesiazousai* are clear, in no sense is Socrates or philosophy at stake in the latter comedy. The comedy of Book V will be treated as a peculiarly Platonic one, in which the self-reflection of philosophy is always at play with the comic elements. It is easier to see how a certain playful ridiculousness functions as an integral part of philosophical reflection where the inspired component is integrated into the movement of questioning.

Socrates announces the incipient comedy when he prostrates himself before the Adrasteia (451a4–5), wards off fear of the jests of the clever (*ton charienton skommatta* [452b7]), and begs these men "not to mind their own business, but to be serious." (452c5–6) The business of the jokers, like Aristophanes, is to ridicule what is ridiculous. Since minding one's own business is the recently established account of justice (443c8–d7), he is asking the jokers to act unjustly. In other words, it is unjust to take the three waves of Book V as serious proposals; they are comic by nature. Socrates' prostration before the daughters of Nemesis admits and presages the excessive speech to follow. But the excess is comic, treating human nature as if it were not bound at all to the condition of embodiment.

A brief treatment of one major aspect of each of the three waves—(1) the two sexes sharing all things, including naked gymnastic, in common (2) the mating of the best with the best, and (3) the philosopher-king—will make this clear. In terms of a reason with the power to overcome the pull of bodily *erōs*, there is nothing objectionable about the proposal of the first wave. But it is precisely because of the pull of *erōs* between the sexes and out of respect for the power of that pull that men and women clothe in the first place. The comedy of the proposal is not in their mutual nakedness. Nothing in the concept of mutual nakedness precludes any sort of mixing in any activities of life. The comedy lies in the underlying presumption that merely through respectful attention to "what is best as revealed in *logoi*" (452d5–6) can the strong and distracting pull of *erōs* between the sexes be overcome. The earlier treatment of Alcibiades' role in the *Symposium* exhibited the powerful claims of the body even in the face of the most exalted *logos*, a claim that is comically absent here.

But another part of the comedy associated with the first wave, which proposes the determination of the nature of the human soul entirely apart from gender, reveals a more serious claim. Where the previous part of the comedy disclosed a difference in terms of the pull of bodies which is comically effaced, this part discloses an affinity which is not ridiculous at all, but courageously creative: the common nature (*phusis*) of men and women in terms of the capabilities of their souls. While *erōs* may escape human control on account of the pull of the body, and while professional skill might not be the sole determinant of the soul's nature, proficiency in an art (*technē*) surely can bring men and women together in the same milieu and on an equal footing. There is nothing preventing men and women from, for example, working together as doctors:

> . . .a man and a woman whose souls are skilled in the doctor's art have the same nature. Or don't you suppose so?   I do.
> But a man doctor and a man carpenter have completely different ones?
> Of course, entirely different. (454c7–d6)

Whether or not a male doctor and carpenter have *completely* different natures is clearly open to question. Again, the pull of the body—here, the similarity of male bodies and their natural functions such as fathering serve as the comic underpinning—serves a comic function. But the comedy clearly opens up the mutual participation of men and women in arts (*technai*) based upon a shared orientation of *soul* as a real possibility in the *Republic*.

The second wave—the belonging together of men and women in common—confounds erotic and geometric necessities, also confounds the divine and the human, and so enlarges the comedy.

> '. . .[T]he most beneficial marriages are to be sacred.' 'That's entirely certain.' (458e4–5)

The best are to mate with the best in order to preserve the quality of humanity in the city. But the "sacred marriage" is the marriage of Hera and Zeus, who were brother and sister. The consequences for incest on the level of the divine are the same as the consequences for everything else: there are no serious and lasting ones at all. But on the human level, the consequences are dreadful: an almost certain and dramatic deterioration in the quality of the lineage. But this is precisely what would happen if mating were managed so that the best always mated with the best in prime years. So deterioration will occur either through incest, or through mating the best with less than the best. The pretense that shrewd (i.e. lie-driven) genetic engineering can preserve the health of the city is comic, playfully forgetting the erotic necessities of the human body.

Unlike the first wave, in which the human soul was considered in its capacity apart from both natural and conventional bonds, the second wave leaves no corresponding surplus in the play of the dialogues. As it occurs entirely on the level of the city and upon the inexorable calculus of the bodies within it, its accompanying seriousness is nothing other than the inevitable decline of cities which the comedy playfully conceals. (The inevitable deterioration of the cities is a theme in Books VIII-IX.)

The third wave, the philosopher-king, has already been discussed extensively in Chapter 5. That the philosopher must always strive for truth, while the king must tell many lies for the sake of his city, indicates the impossibility in its very conception of such a figure. It is a comic impossibility because even beyond this logical impossibility (and beyond the comedy of hoping that the two opposed natures could somehow "fall together" (*sumpesē*) after all of the planning),[126] the same recalcitrance of the body discussed in connection with the first two waves would assert itself after the installation of the philosopher-king anyway.

The seriousness concealed within this comic impossibility at its heart is the need for the union of wisdom and action, a need which animates Socratic and all genuine philosophical activity. It is a need both of cities and of individual souls. The third wave addresses this union in a profoundly playful manner. What occurs as comic impossibility in the city, namely the impossibility of the philosopher-king, oddly allows for the individual soul's most promising possibility. In cities, the need for wise action cannot be fully met because of the antithetical natures of the philosophic and political natures. When wise actions are performed by statesmen in cities, the actors are not themselves guided by wisdom but by right opinion, which Socrates likens to divination (*Meno* 99b5–c5). But in individual souls, philosophy as love of wisdom makes possible action guided by honest partial insight and its accompanying recognition of ignorance.

The admission of willing lies to the soul destroys its philosophical nature.[127] The "lies" which *are* permitted are *myths*, which can disclose insights inaccessible in other ways. The noble lie of the city cannot be told by a philosopher at all; not only is it a willing lie, but a wholly calculated one. A noble lie which takes its departure from the philosophical life as it tells the inspired tale which founds and supports the soul in this life is another matter. The myth of Er at the end of the *Republic* is the counterpart of the noble lie of the city. The soul is fashioned under the earth in both tales, but only in the myth of Er does the soul learn to choose more wisely through the abiding practice of philosophy. In this way, what occurs as comedy and impossibility in the city opens the way to philosophy as possibility in the individual soul.

There is a symmetry to the treatment of comedy and tragedy. Both can be injurious to souls if they are interpreted as actual proposals issuing from the identification of individual soul and city, rather than as playful and often profound possibilities for the liberated human soul. Both the damage in speech done by Achilles' words from Hades to the guardians-in-training in their city, and the actual damage done by Aristophanes' play to the reputation of Socrates in his, issue from the city-based literal interpretation these works of art were given. According to such literalism, death makes the bravest one tremble and Socrates is a money-seeking fraud. And in both cases, the poetic images disclose the real possibility of a philosophical life when they are interpreted as free creations of and for the wisdom-seeking soul, which is capable of honoring the obligations of citizenship but is also capable of discerning other obligations.

It falls to comedy to laugh at limits or to treat limits as if they did not exist, for example to present Socrates swinging in a basket looking down upon the sun and all earthly things with sublime disdain.[128] Just as tragedy is the best friend of the soul which needs to recollect its limits (including its debt to the city), comedy is the best friend of the soul which would, in seeking new possibilities, transcend those limits (including the ones set by the established practices of the city). In the play of the Platonic dialogues, the philosophical soul befriends both. . .with an ever-so-slight preference for the comic.

PART III

PLAY AND THE SOUL

CHAPTER NINE:
PLAY AND SELF-KNOWLEDGE:
TYPHONIC DESTINY AND
THE WRITTEN WORD

In Plato's *Phaedrus*, Socrates presents the art of writing in a myth in which the usefulness and limits of this art are declared. Writing will neither aid memory nor further the pursuit of wisdom but rather will harm these, producing a forgetfulness of the soul in the first case and a conceit in the second. However, writing can serve as a *pharmakon* (commonly translated as "remedy") which furthers recollection (*anamimnēskomenous*), reminding (*hupomnēseōs*) one of something that has been forgotten. (275a4–5) I will leave *pharmakon* untranslated from here on, for its many senses are at play in the dialogue: drug, remedy, medicine, enchanted potion, charm, spell, enchanting poison. They share a sense of non-rational transport, non-rational agent for change of condition. On the other key words, *mnēmē* and its variants will always be rendered as "memory," *hupomnēsis* and its variants will be rendered as "reminding," and *anamnēsis* and its variants will be rendered as "recollection."

We will now revisit the beginning of Plato's *Phaedrus*,[129] where Socrates is asked by Phaedrus whether he is persuaded of the truth of the myth of Boreas and Oreithuia. After responding that he would be less strange (*atopon*, "without place"[130]) if he followed the wise ones by disbelieving it and by "explaining away" (*sophizomenos*, literally "making wise"; also "dealing craftily"), he says that he lacks the leisure to explain away a host of "impossible," mythical beings because

> I am not yet able to know myself, in accord with the Delphic oracle. And it seems ridiculous to me to study various other matters when I am ignorant of this one. Therefore regarding them I am persuaded by the customary view, studying not them but myself—do I happen to be a wild beast more convoluted and more passionate than Typhon, or a tamer and simpler animal, with a nature given an un-Typhonic destiny by the gods? (229e5–230a7)

The task of self-knowledge presented in this passage is not one among others, but determines and rules all other tasks. Together with this, Socrates affirms his ignorance of his own nature, not knowing whether it is Typhonic or un-Typhonic, the most monstrous or something more gentle. Nor is any attempt made to explain away something dark. There is no move to replace a myth with a learned explanation; Socrates refuses to remake a tale of love and divinity into a rational account of natural causes. The ground of this refusal is not said to be the falsity of the "fashionable" answer (nothing is said about this one way or the other). Nor does Socrates decline to rationalize the myths out of an innocent belief in their truth (he calls the actual existence of the mythical beings, who he calls *amēchanon*—impossible, in the sense of unconstructable). Rather, he declines to rationalize the myths because of the irrelevance of this activity to the task of self-knowledge. Accounts which would explain the past as a series of more or less inconsequential occurrences, ordained by natural causes of some sort, simply have no place on the pathway to self-knowledge. But Typhon is given a prominent place on Socrates' path.

Typhon, child of Gē and Tartarus, and arguably the vilest, ugliest monster in all Greek mythology, won his fame by challenging and nearly subduing Zeus, having successfully bound the Olympian king and having cut the tendons of his arms and wrists. Hermes then fooled Typhon into falling asleep, and made the necessary repairs on Zeus' limbs.[131] How might Socrates, of all figures, be seen as having a Typhonic destiny?

Typhon is the creature capable of the greatest *hubris*, the greatest transgression of limits. He is the one who would assault and destroy what is highest and best. One becomes Typhonic, then, by forgetting one's limits and transgressing them. In employing Typhon's destiny as a vicarious image by treating it as a factor in the questioning of his own destiny, Socrates acknowledges the possibility of forgetting and transgressing his own limits. Thus through the image of a very old mythical figure, Socrates reminds himself of this possibility and thereby keeps in mind the need not to exceed his limits. In other words, he keeps open the possibility of an un-Typhonic destiny. In this way, the tale is not simply a story of a non-existent past but of a living possibility which is always present and always at play. It offers something most useful for the future: a vivid image which serves as a reminder to act in accord with, and in a way which does no violence to, what is highest and best.

In this indirect manner, which does not explicitly proclaim his belief in the truth of the myth (and calls its figures "impossible") but which vicariously enters into mythical imagery, Socrates gives an affirmative answer to Phaedrus' question: he believes in the truth of what the myth shows. While he does not say that the tale it tells has actually occurred (for it lies beyond any kind of verification, and that is not its domain[132]), he shows the way in which an old tale can serve as a true guide in the proper performance of the task of self-knowledge.

However, the guidance to life which the myth provides makes sense only if the condition of the one guided is acknowledged self-ignorance: only then are Typhonic and un-Typhonic destinies, *hubris* and measure, both possible at every moment. The *pharmakon* of writing recalls the way an old spoken tale can enchant its hearer to a properly measured life, allowing a non-rational and archaic source to function as a call to the soul in the present for the sake of a possible future. In this way, the destiny of Typhon becomes part of a future for the self: by reminding it to be mindful of its limits, the image of this destiny serves as a reminder of the ills which can fall to an ignorant being, and so provides a possibility of remedy from and for them.

Taking this back one more step, the Platonic dialogues themselves are writings which remind the soul of its need for myths as well as arguments in its pursuit of wisdom. *Mythos* and *logos*, related to one another and to the deeds recounted in the dialogues, comprise a mutually reflective and tightly woven tapestry in which each part is picked up and reflected in the others (see Chapter 6 above). I have called these tapestry-like qualities, both rule-governed and inspired, the play of the Platonic dialogues. The Socrates/Typhon interplay, in which both rational and non-rational elements intertwine for the sake of a self-knowledge to which both light and darkness belong, exemplifies this play—which the reader may enter vicariously.

But there is another way of regarding this play, namely as unbound to any structure, as occurring "beyond man and humanism," and as traceable in certain aspects of writing. This view of play is offered as a possibility liberating humanity from the constraints of Western metaphysics. In Plato, this play is said to be both saved and suppressed. These are the views of Jacques Derrida.[133] In order both to set off the views offered here from those of Derrida, and to preserve the genuine playfulness of Platonic writing from the intrusions upon it visited by this clever and influential but misguided critic who—perhaps out of friendship, perhaps not—would submerge it beneath alien concerns, I digress from the exposition and offer a critique of Derrida's "Plato's Pharmacy." The exposition will resume directly after it.

* *

"Plato's Pharmacy" is the second and longest of three pieces in Jacques Derrida's *Dissemination*.[134] The piece directs itself explicitly toward the theme of writing, culminates in a section on play, and treats many of the same issues and focuses upon many of the same passages as the ones treated here. Despite some similarity to my general orientation to the history of philosophy and some admiration for the acuteness with which he locates and exploits key texts, I find myself in strong dissent with both the nature and the specifics of Derrida's interpretation of Platonic writing, Platonic play and associated matters. I will select several issues at which our interests converge, but not our outcomes.

1) Recollection: for Derrida, the ability of writing to provoke recollection is taken to mean recall of what is already "inscribed" in the soul, the "forms" or *eidē*.

> Live memory repeats the presence of the *eidos*, and truth is then also the possibility of repetition through recall. . .The true is the presence of the *eidos* signified.[135]

But in the discussion of the Typhon in the *Phaedrus*, the recollective process provoked by the written word need not be a recollection of the *eidē* at all! No *eidos* occurs in the recollection of the myth of Typhon, but rather one is reminded to bear in mind the appropriate measure for a human being, who is given over to darkness in an essential way. This image and this reflection upon it are quite enough for Socrates' substantial insight into his own soul without any recourse to *eidē*. Still further, given the bond to images and sensation (*aisthēsis*) which has been repeatedly established in this book, such recollection is never of the *eidē* in any direct sense.

2) Writing[136]: for all his supposed radicality and sensitivity to the playfulness and essential undecidability of textual meaning, Derrida moves within a fairly traditional and static notion of Platonism. Accordingly, the dominant strain is seen as rationalistic and dualistic—although another strain works against it at its heart.

> Plato thinks of writing, and tries to comprehend it, to dominate it, on the basis of *opposition* as such. In order for these contrary values (good/evil, true/false, essence/appearance, inside/outside, etc.) to be in opposition, each of the terms must be simply *external* to the other, which means that one of the oppositions (the opposition between inside and outside) must already be accredited as the matrix of all oppositions.[137]

In the dominant strain, writing is the outside of what is inside the soul; just as appearance is the outside in relation to *eidos*. But in the other strain, writing as *pharmakon* can enchant and bewitch. This non-rational power threatens the structure of the system of oppositions it inhabits.

But there is nothing in Plato which asserts, argues for or in any way points to a dominant rationalistic strain, an "inside" versus an "outside" or a system of oppositions of any kind. First of all, it is always useful to recall Sallis' reminders that there may be no philosophy of Plato[138] and that "Plato never says anything."[139] Thus to speak of Plato as agent or as holder of views (e.g. "Plato thinks"), as Derrida is given to do, is questionable at the very least. Among the worst passages is the following: "One must indeed be aware of the fact that Plato is suspicious of the *pharmakon* in general [even when it is therapeutic in every sense]. . .The *pharmakon* can never be simply beneficial."[140] To say that in the Platonic texts *pharmakon* can heal as well as harm is to say one thing, although nothing very interesting; to say that on this basis it is a settled matter that Plato is suspicious of the *pharmakon* is to say quite another, namely that his observation of alternative directions of the *pharmakon* bears witness to a certain attitude of Plato toward it. With this and other such proclamations, Derrida clearly presupposes the same interpretation of inside/outside (i.e. Plato's mental state/Plato's writing) that he purports to discover in Plato. This interpretive misstep can be traced to its source.

Derrida's Plato-interpretation, like this one, has been influenced in important ways by Heidegger's approach to Greek thought. Such readings engage the whole of the Greek text as a living thing (as *Phaedrus* 264c2–3 reflectively suggests), not merely as a repository of arguments of varying merits. Heidegger's gift to the reception of Plato is not his positive readings, but his unpeeling of centuries of sedimented accretions of philosophically alien concerns from the Platonic texts so that they could be encountered in their own way of philosophizing. However one may regard his readings of individual dialogues and his treatment of Plato as a whole, he provided the inestimably valuable service of putting to rout much that had been mistakenly taken for granted. Based on a reading of the dialogues on their own terms, one finds neither concepts or consciousness in Plato (there is no Greek word which can, without substantial elucidation, be translated by either); in the same terms, there is no social or political philosophy or ethics or aesthetics, nor any theories or teachings. If we are to hear Plato, we must let the Platonic text speak from itself in all of its power.

None of this means that Plato was unconcerned with the areas of experience we have come to associate with "concepts," "consciousness," society/politics and art. Rather, these matters which now are sectioned off into specialties and accorded their own vocabularies and methodologies were treated in the dialogues as belonging to the web of human questioning within which the sole aim was human wisdom, and the abiding orientations were the dimly beheld *eidē* on one side and the recognition of ignorance upon the other. It may seem legitimate to import such notions as consciousness or concept and its object, or ideas of ethical, social or political norms, or axiological and ontological concerns of art into Plato on the grounds that these importations are natural extensions of Platonic (and indeed of all) philosophical thought and that the dialogues themselves function much in the way our contemporary philosophical specialties do. But the dialogues do not function in this way. Introducing such concerns into the dialogues can easily lead to distorting what they say as well as how they philosophize.

How astonishing such an attitude seemed, and how liberating once put into practice! The reader of Plato who had trouble reconciling the received wisdom of Platonic intellectualism with the prominent non-rational strains in the dialogue was shown a possibility of thinking the two together, but had to fashion that possibility through the work of interpreting the dialogues anew. This work has hardly begun, and the explorations of Platonic play in this book contribute to that work.

However, one of the principal outcomes of this interpretive tradition which begins in Heidegger and features itself prominently in Derrida has become an impediment to that work, and now functions as a new accretion at odds with everything that has been said about liberating the Platonic dialogues from alien concerns. I refer to the casting of Plato as the voice of the dawn of Western metaphysics, as the site of the decline of thought into whatever it is said to decline into: from concern with Being to busying oneself with beings, from thought to philosophy, from experience of the primordial to the second-order conception of dualisms, from letting-be to dominance/submissiveness, et al. Let me say at once that I take these issues seriously and that, in the case of Heidegger, I regard them as great thoughts and crucial to the releasing of previously untapped resources in our tradition. They issue from an analysis of truth in Plato which retains both its richness and its force.

In "Plato's Doctrine of Truth," Heidegger speaks of two strains on truth in Plato's cave image: truth as unhiddenness (*a-lētheia*), the originary Greek sense of truth; and truth as "enslaving [unhiddenness] beneath the *idea*."[141] (The German word which I rendered as "enslaving," *unterjochen*, literally means "under-yoking" and recalls *Republic* 507e6–508a1, where Socrates discusses the yoking (*suzeuxeōn*) of the sense of sight with the power of being by the measure of an *idea*.) Although Plato's transformation, in terms of which what is true receives its measure of truth from the degree of its manifestation in terms of the *idea* is decisive for the cave image and for the Platonic dialogues, "unhiddenness also retains a rank."[142]   I wish to emphasize that while Heidegger certainly leans toward interpreting Plato out of the second strain in which the *idea* is seen as decisive and as giving rise to the history of rationalism (with truth as clear and distinct idea as one of its most important formulations), the first strain in which truth occurs as originary ongoing movement of disclosure and concealment is always present. In the language of this book, the two are always at play, and have been most succinctly presented as the ongoing intertwining and non-intersecting of *mythos* and *logos*.

For Heidegger, the orientation in terms of the *idea* moves away from the originary experience of truth (hidden-unhidden) toward the derivative dualism of true and false, and toward kindred dualisms which pervade the history of philosophy. But when one seeks to locate these dualisms and dodges in Plato, they cannot be found any more than rationalism and intellectualism can be found. Despite Heidegger's own cautions, he views the dialogues from time to time as documents to be studied as clues to the vagaries of our history, and not as living conversations. Derrida's treatment goes further: the dialogues are often little more than symptom-bearing specimens.

Let us consider several examples:

But the fact that 'Platonism', which sets up the whole of Western metaphysics in its conceptuality, should not escape the generality of this structural constraint [i.e. 'assign{ing} the origin and power of speech, precisely of *logos*, to the "paternal position"] and even illustrates it with incomparable subtlety and force, stands out as all the more significant.[143]

It [i.e. the bringing out of the structural resemblance between the Platonic and the other mythological figures of the origin of writing] must open onto the general problematic of the relations between mythemes and the philosophemes that lie at the heart of Western *logos*. That is to say of a history—or rather of History—which has been produced in its entirety in the *philosophical* difference between *mythos* and *logos*, blindly sinking down into that difference as the natural obviousness of its own element.[144]

And if the network of opposing predicates that link one type of writing to the other [i.e. good to bad, linked through the opposing predicates of, e.g., "knowledgeable" and "ignorant"] contains in its meshes all the conceptual oppositions of Platonism—here considered the dominant structure of the history of metaphysics—then it can be said that philosophy is played out in the play between two kinds of writing.[145]

Regarding such extravagant proclamations concerning "the *whole* of Western metaphysics in its conceptuality," of a "History" "produced *entirely* in the philosophical difference between *mythos* and *logos*," and about "*all* the conceptual oppositions in Plato" [emphases on "whole," "entirely" and "all" are mine], it is enough to note that there is no accounting by Derrida for the possibility of a standpoint from which one can survey and determine the wholeness, entirety and allness of anything—except perhaps from that of the straw man of "Western metaphysics" he is attempting to expose and undermine. Further, many of his key words also presuppose the oppositions he ascribes to the straw man: "sets up" in the first citation; "lie at the heart" in the second; "dominant structure" in the third.

But the issue is Plato. What has Plato to do with "assigning *logos* to the paternal position," and with "conceptuality"? With the "philosophical difference between *mythos* and *logos*" at the heart of a history which is blind to this difference? With conceptual oppositions, which are somehow played out in writing? The answer in terms of the dialogues is (charitably) very little or (less charitably) nothing. As even Derrida concedes, the assignment of origin to a father is not confined to Plato; of course, it is hardly remarkable at all. But to say that the power of *logos* derives from the "paternal position" (the move from "father" serving as an image in Plato to a "paternal position" in Plato is a vast interpretive intrusion) is quite simply false in addition to being trivial, and directly refuted not only by the midwife image in the *Theaetetus* but by Diotima in the *Symposium* and by the priestess in the *Apology* who told Chaerophon that no one was wiser than Socrates.

Further, the view that the location of all power of speech issues from the male in Greek culture can be refuted by even a superficial reading of the Homeric poems. That Derrida might try to make some large point about the metaphoricity of the Western soul is, of course, legitimate. But his use of Plato to make that point fails. And again, the attribution of "conceptuality" to Plato also fails, or at least requires a much deeper tale than Derrida tells. There is no Greek word in Plato which does the work of our "concept," and the notion of a real separation of ideas from images does not occur in the dialogues, as this work has been at pains to show.

With this, both Derrida's *mythos/logos* difference and his "conceptual oppositions" which constitute Platonism as the "dominant structure in the history of metaphysics" also are exposed as interpretive intrusions comprised of one small part of the Platonic texts mixed with a large quantity of externally derived predeterminations concerning Plato, concerning "Platonism" and concerning so-called Western metaphysics. As we have seen throughout this book and particularly in Chapter 6, *mythos* and *logos* always occur as inextricably intertwined in the dialogues. It is their separation and sharp differentiation that is resisted time after time. Those "oppositions" noted by Derrida may occur, but they are neither "constitutive" nor "dominant." They arise and recede in service to the ignorance-acknowledging pursuit of wisdom, and never superimpose themselves upon that pursuit for long. The soul, recognizing ignorance but erotically directed toward the good, is the abiding presence in the Platonic dialogues. Play in the face of the bond to images, not metaphysical conviction, is its abiding comportment.

With respect to the issue of play in Plato, Derrida uses a different tactic. He notes Plato's praise of play, but also the conditional nature of this praise. Play is praised " 'in the best sense of the word,' if this can be said without eliminating play beneath the reassuring silliness of such a precaution." Such precautions, which involve its lawfulness, are "the safeguards of ethics and politics."[146] He interprets the key passage from the *Laws*, in which the play of sacrificing, singing and dancing is called the right way of living,[147] as calling for a play seeking salvation in "games," and calls such play "lost."[148] But such unfettered play might well threaten the edifice of Platonism from within itself.

Again, Derrida's interpretation reveals a good deal about the interests of the interpretation, namely to overcome the ambiguity in Platonic play and arrive at a "found" play free of precautions. And again, the interpretation misses the dialogues it would encounter to further this end. The notion that play is most properly itself apart from measure is nowhere defended and certainly has no place in the Platonic dialogues (see Chapter 1 above). Even the playing child of Heraclitus does not "merely play" but plays at draughts (*pais esti paizon, pesseuon*[149]), a game in which chance has a role but which is rule-governed and finite in its possibilities.

Derrida, a writer who discovers playful connections in the dialogues as readily and exploits them as astutely as anyone, misses the fundamental playfulness of the dialogues. The "oppositions" and "subordinations" and "structures" he discovers do not "constitute" the dialogue but occur at play within it. And when they speak of those elements which *are* constitutive, such as writing and of play, the dialogues do not attempt to master or subdue these in any way. Rather, they open up a distance between the written word and what it calls forth, and between the playfulness and what is at stake in the play. The reader, then, is not surveying a specimen of philosophy's history or receiving and perhaps weighing opinions, but entering into the movement of the dialogue. The self-reflection of writing and of play in the dialogues opens the possibility for a certain kind of philosophical encounter with the self-reflection of the reader.

When Derrida says, "play and art are lost by Plato as he saves them. . .,"[150] he misses this self-reflection, mistaking it for a desire to dominate or tame them. Despite his sensitivity to the dramatic elements of the Platonic texts, he regards these texts not on their own terms but as founding documents in the history of Western metaphysics—a residue of Heidegger which has done as much good and as much harm (especially here) as any interpretive insight of the century. Neither Derrida nor anyone else has such a handle, or any other kind of handle, on Plato. There is no handle for anyone on the Platonic dialogues. If there is a handle, it is theirs upon us.

* *

The words of the myth of writing say: ". . .[The people's trust in writing will] not provoke their recollection from within themselves through themselves. Not for memory but for reminding have you discovered a *pharmakon*." (". . .*ouk endothen autous huph' autōn anamimnēskomenous. Oukoun mnēmēs alla hupomnēseōs pharmakon ēures*.") (275a4–6) There are three tiers of inner search spoken of in this short passage: (1) memory (*mnēmē*) or straightforward recall of the past, an ability damaged by writing, which made it less needed and therefore less practiced; (2) reminding (*hupomnēsis*), as externally provoking recall of something now out of one's attention but which was once present to it; (3) recollection (*anamnēsis*), recall out of oneself of something forgotten.

Mere memory involves no account; no *logos* is given of what is recalled. There is a mere reproducing of what was presented earlier. Recollection involves at least the possibility of such an account, since the knowledge was generated within oneself. (Thus every *anamnēsis* can produce what *mnēmē* has accomplished, but not conversely.) Writing can cause a breakdown in *mnēmē*; but interpreted playfully, the myth says that writing has already done so, that memory has already been weakened by it. So, too, has recollection. A good part of the *Phaedrus* has been occupied with the issue of the pernicious influence of written speeches, which mislead their listeners into accepting what they otherwise might know or discover that they should reject.

Reminding (*hupomnēsis*) occurs where there is a breakdown either in memory (*mnēmē*) or in recollection (*anamnēsis*). While *hupomnēsis* can serve either *mnēmē* or *anamnēsis*, the next part of the myth which Socrates relates stresses its potential damage to the philosophical interest: "and you offer to your disciples the appearance of wisdom, not true wisdom." (275a6–7) True wisdom, insofar as it can be discerned from the Platonic dialogues, requires self-confrontation by the human being of his/her own limits, e.g. through the sort of recollection enacted by Socrates with the aid of the Typhon myth discussed above. The ordinary function of memory can be fully served by the reminding which occurs through writing, in the way that a book can when certain passages in it are sought, or a shopping list can when the needed items slip one's mind. But clearly recollection can not be so served, and in this case the writing can merely provoke the activity of self-confrontation, which must draw upon the inner resources of the human being in order to be completed.

But writing provokes in the manner of a *pharmakon*. It displaces, removes, sets the usual everyday reality at a distance and so makes possible an encounter with something other than the everyday. The *pharmakon* might serve an aim of sophistry, or it might serve as a reminder which leads to a genuine recollection. For the latter, the soul in its forgetfulness must already be disposed toward the kind of recollection which requires its genuine participation, and so the character of the writing is not the only issue in the recollection. The vicarious participation of the soul of Socrates in the myth of Typhon, culminating in the self-questioning of his own nature, shows a soul already given over to measure and a soul whose engagement with the *mythos* is predicated precisely upon a certain distance from the *mythos*. While *pharmakon* can make itself manifest and displace in many ways, the *Phaedrus* celebrates the meeting of *pharmakon* and the forgetful but philosophically disposed soul.

But what does it mean to say that a soul is "philosophically disposed?" How can the soul be latently disposed toward recollection and what it discloses, only to forget this disposition and its inclination? According to the myth of Theuth and Thamus, the mere existence and prevalence of the art of writing is one cause: the laziness of soul brought about by writing begets flaccidity in its own resources of memory, which is the necessary condition of all self-reflection. The habit of writing becomes the habit of non-remembering, silently but surely eviscerating the muscles of memory in even the most philosophically oriented soul. But in Socrates' second speech, the soul which seeks true wisdom is shown to have a mixture of recollection and forgetfulness built into its nature. In other words, the divinely mad, erotic, philosophically oriented soul is also a soul which is disposed to forget—and forgetfulness is hardly restricted to items on a list.

All four forms of divine madness in the hymn to *Erōs* introduce measure into the realms they enter. The oracles of prophetesses and priestesses bring measure to action and life (e.g. the *gnosi seauton* of the priestess at Delphi); the healing of illnesses restores proper measure to the body; the tragedies fashioned under the guidance of the Muses sing the measure of human beings and gods; and *Erōs* restrains the downward-tending desires "and liberat[es] that which belongs to virtue." (256b3) This madness, a dark non-rational impulse, reigns at the source of the soul's philosophical disposition. The conceit of a soul which believes it knows what it does not issues from the forgetfulness of this darkness; the belief that the soul has the measure extinguishes the darkness. The soul animated by philosophical *erōs*, when it encounters writing as *pharmakon* for reminding, is impelled toward the deed of recollection which is its proper act and which includes recollection of the darkness to which it is partially but essentially given over.

The great myth of the gods steering their chariots to the outer reaches of the heavens and feasting on pure being, while the human beings trailing behind gain a mere glimpse of what the gods see, is an event in writing which provokes recollection of the human soul's destiny:

> For a soul which has never seen the truth cannot pass into human form. For a
> human being must understand how to bring together according to *eidos*, collecting
> into a one by means of reasoning (*logismo*) out of the many sensations; and this
> is a recollection of what the soul once beheld (*eiden*) when it. . .lifted up into
> beingly being (*on ontōs*). (249b6–c6)

Disembodied human souls once beheld pure being in "pure light" (250c4), but now the prison of the body keeps us at a distance from what we once saw. Losing ourselves in bodily pleasures, we would forget this vision. But beauty provokes the recollection. Taking the great myth together with the myth of writing, the writing of the conversation between Phaedrus and Socrates provokes the doubled recollection (i.e. the recollection of the recollection) of the *eidē* of which Socrates speaks. And taking the written provocation of the recollection one step further back, the mythical nature of the original seeing together with the return from the bodily things to the *eidē* establishes human seeing as an incomplete and partially dark seeing of the *eidē*. In this way, the second-order activity of writing mirrors the second-order experience of the *eidē* for humans.

This dimming down of the recollection of the *eidē* is not imposed from the soul of the seeker. Nor is it imposed by "reason" or "will" or any of its surrogates. Nor do the gods impose it by means of divine madness. The self-measuring of the recollection belongs to the movement of the human soul itself, which knows that it has a glimmer of more than it actually knows, but that this sighting of the *eidē* is no more than a glimmer. (This is why, throughout the dialogues, the *eidē* and their employment occur in arguments in which their sense is generally understood, although no direct exhibition of them is ever offered or said to be witnessed.) The myth presents the movement of the philosophically oriented soul in a vicarious image, in which the most powerful *erōs* joins with the most powerful sense of measure.[151] What is forgotten in forgetfulness is not merely the *eidē*, but the *eidē* together with the measure of their sighting—and further forgotten is the measure this recollection imposes upon the would-be seer both in thought and in action. The greatest orientation toward virtue coupled with the most vigorous restraint (on the hubristic horse[152]) toward chastity are the product of the most intensely mad *erōs*. It is clear in the myth that the recovery of measure is just as important to the health of the human soul as the sighting of the *eidē*, and that the orientation toward virtue is one with the generation of measure.[153]

How, then, does writing function in the Platonic dialogues? Regarded in a structural way, it can be seen merely as a general reminder, a surrogate for second-order experience in general. Regarded as reminder of a living *logos*, it can elicit the reflective, vicarious participation of the soul. Writing occurs neither as subordinate to *logos* (in the way that an image might be unreflectively regarded as subordinate to its original), nor does it occur as an indeterminate *pharmakon* undermining pre-existing structures (as if writing functioned apart from the play of elements in which it occurs). The humanly contrived written speeches of Lysias and the divinely inspired myth of Typhon are both written and both redirect the soul. Their difference in the dialogue does not derive, then, from their being written nor from their power to engage the soul. It derives from what they say, and from how the soul responds to that saying.

So no definite inferences about a *logos* can be made based upon the premise that it is written, only that the play of memory, forgetfulness and recollection belongs to it. The great myth, written into the dialogue, can insert itself into the movement of recollection/forgetfulness of the reader, who can take it up in writing, speech or silence. The *Phaedrus* itself functions playfully as recollection-provoking *pharmakon*. It is a written dialogue about writing, a *pharmakon* about *pharmakonoi*. On many levels it playfully enacts the playful recoil it would provoke in a soul on the path to self-knowledge, but never without the soul's own participation.

CHAPTER TEN:
DAIMONION AT PLAY

If the Platonic texts are taken on their own terms, one cannot fail to note the association of the *daimonion* and its accompanying phenomena with *mythos*. *Daimōn*, the word from which its "diminuitive" *daimonion* derives, almost always refers in the dialogues to a divinity located between gods and men, mediating the traffic.[154] The clearest expression of this mediation occurs in the *Symposium*. In the myth told by the mythical Diotima to Socrates, a *daimōn* "interprets and conveys things to the gods from human beings and from human beings to the gods. . . .Since it is in the middle it fills in between the two so that the whole is bound together by it." (202e3–7) This location between the human and divine realms is the first essential aspect of the daimonic.

The second principal aspect, related to the first but having a separate significance, concerns its location beyond the everyday human realm. The ironic interjection *"O daimones!"* aptly indicates that its target has said or done something beyond what is appropriate for a human being. At *Republic* 344d6, Socrates calls Thrasymachus *"O daimonie. . ."* for trying to leave after attempting to overwhelm his interlocutors with an invective-rich argument which held injustice to be more valuable than justice. At *Republic*

509c1–2, Glaucon targets Socrates, who just declared the good to be "beyond being," for speaking with "daimonic excess."[155] Both aspects—the mythical location between gods and humans and beyond the customarily human—are characteristic of the *daimonion* of Socrates, which accordingly inspires uncustomary responses.

Although its appearance is relatively infrequent, the *daimonion* must be accorded important status[156]. It binds Socrates to his most important tasks and surfaces at crucial moments in the performance of those tasks. Unlike the *daimōn* spoken of in the myth of Diotima, there is no ongoing two-way exchange of sacrifices and entreaties to the gods for commands and gifts from them. There is, however, an exchange which occurs through the Socratic *daimonion*: the self-questioning and self-measuring it provokes makes possible the ongoing exchange of wondering ignorance for better insight, of greater folly for greater human wisdom. Whereas the daimonic traffic is presented as purposefully directive and directed, the *daimonion* of Socrates never instructs him or urges him forward but only restrains him, leading him to consider a detour from the course he was following. Its absence grants permission to proceed as he had been doing. (*Apology* 40b1–6) There is no positive content to the *daimonion*, just a flash which interrupts and provokes, and so grants the possibility of the aforementioned philosophical exchange.

In this sense, the *daimonion* returns Socrates to the pathway of self-questioning, bringing him back to the play of rational and non-rational sources and to his own power of inquiry and response within that play. The very idea of a non-directive signal which arrives out of the dark in order to provoke the shedding of light suggests its fundamental orientation toward play. However, it has not often been seen in this way. Often, the *daimonion* is interpreted as a conscience or special instinct. Just as in the case of Derrida[157] in the previous chapter on the issues of writing and *pharmakon*, Hegel has addressed the issue of the Socratic *daimonion* in an intensive and powerful manner which rewards direct engagement. Hegel imports his own concerns into the Platonic dialogues, with often surprising and insightful results. But he distorts and submerges the philosophical experience most proper to an encounter with the dialogues. For this reason, a second digression will examine the brilliant distortions of the Hegelian view of the Socratic *daimonion*, in order to allow the latter to shine forth more clearly from its own setting.

Like Derrida, Hegel is *serious*. His work takes Plato seriously. Plato is interpreted as an important moment in the history of rational self-consciousness, just as for Derrida the dialogues are founding texts in the history of Western metaphysics. The dialogues can be temporarily drowned out in either neighborhood. But after these neighborhoods are visited and their environs properly surveyed, one can find exits from their noisier districts (if not from the neighborhoods themselves). Then one can rejoin the play of the Platonic dialogues.

* *

With impeccable correctness, Hegel notes that the Socratic *daimonion* is not a function of reason. But insofar as he regards it as an instinct which serves the rational interest (however blindly), one would think that Hegel would find the *daimonion* of Socrates to be a clear precursor of the modern conscience. This is not the case. To understand the *daimonion* (which Hegel calls Socrates' *Genius*), "we are neither to image the existence of a protective spirit, angel, and such like, nor even of conscience. For conscience is the idea of universal individuality, of the mind certain of itself, which is at the same time universal truth."[158] This negative characterization is driven by Socrates' insistence upon the peculiarity of the *daimonion* to him, a claim made in several places and very clearly at *Republic* 496c4, and *Apology* 31c7–d6.

In his positive formulation, Hegel says that "the Genius of Socrates is rather all the other and necessary sides of his universality, that is, the individuality of mind which came to consciousness in him equally with the former."[159] The sundering of the *daimonion* from pure consciousness and the true universality of mind arises from its coming forth as "*unconscious impulse*."[160] Where the Hegelian conscience unites pure consciousness and individuality in an act of conviction, the Socratic *daimonion* manifests itself suddenly, out of the dark, and at a time of decision. For Hegel the "out of the dark" means: from outside. He places emphasis upon how much Greek decision-making relied upon non-rational outside forces: "For in making these decisions, the Greeks took refuge in oracles, sacrificial animals, soothsayers or, like the Romans, asked counsel of birds in flight."[161] This element, that "the people were determined from without," showed that the time was not yet present for them to recognize the inward freedom and independence (and hence responsibility) which would both allow and enable them to decide for themselves on rational grounds. Or in another, telling formulation: "[t]he Greeks did not possess the knowledge of this infinitude."[162]

According to Hegel, infinite and finite are presented as separate in the Socratic *daimonion*. Socrates was not without consciousness of his infinitude, but this infinitude was merely his pure thought. For Hegel, this pure thought gives knowledge of what is universal, and universal knowledge alone is knowledge of the essential. Mere particular cases are trivial and therefore are untouched by pure thought. For such particular cases divination is necessary, and these are the only matters over which the *daimonion* holds sway: "[T]he truly divine and universal is the institution of agriculture, the state, marriage, etc.; compared to this it is a trivial matter to know whether, when I go out to sea, I shall perish or not."[163] The *daimonion* may be seen as an unconscious filling up of the gap of pure consciousness. In this sense, it is "outside" pure consciousness.

One must admire both the depth and the subtlety of Hegel's analysis. The *daimonion* can be (significantly) likened neither to the Hegelian conscience nor to its precursor in the Kantian categorical imperative with its allied conscience. It has no direct connection to any sort of rational law, much less an inward, self-governing law. Like conscience, the *daimonion* tacitly empowers the individual, granting a certain right to determine his/her action according to a measure other than that of the state or church or family. But this misses what is peculiar to the Hegelian/Kantian conscience, namely its connection to the universal concept of duty which gives authoritative sanction to its claim (in its positive aspect).

When the Platonic dialogues of Socrates are interpreted without the

Hegelian/modern cast over them, we can see how much this cast confines them. In the Greek, we see no word which evolves into our *Pflicht* or "duty," no word for "consciousness" or "concept," and even those words which we translate as "universal" (*katholou*) and "particular" (*hekastos*) do not have the same abstract significance that we give them.

> The Genius of Socrates moreover reveals itself in him through nothing other than the counsel given respecting these particular issues, such as when and whether his friends ought to travel. To anything true, existing in and for itself in art or in science, he made no reference, for that pertains to the universal mind, and these daimonic revelations are thus much more unimportant than those of his thinking mind.[164]

For a thinker who has written about Socrates with penetration and insight that is often remarkable, Hegel's is a stunning misrepresentation of the *daimonion* of Socrates. While he correctly notes that it stands between "the eternality of the oracle and the pure inwardness of mind," it is false to say either that the *daimonion* comes forth only in trivialities which concern the particular fate of individuals, or that the revelations of the *daimonion* were of a lower order than those of "art or science."[165]

The voice from childhood described by Socrates in the famous passage of the *Apology* (31d1–6), which always dissuades but never urges on to action, surely directs the individual Socrates to make particular decisions. But these decisions are never trivial, nor are they merely concerned with the outcome of an individual choice. For Socrates they are always concerned not with art of science in the Hegelian sense, but with the activity of *philosophy*. Though Hegel would overcome this in his *Phenomenology of Spirit* ("the goal that philosophy be able to set aside its name of *love* of *knowing* and to be *actual knowing*—is the one I set for myself"[166]), this is clearly not the Socratic project.

In the *Apology*, the *daimonion* restrains Socrates from participating in public life, and is silent while he speaks so uncompromisingly to his accusers and fellow citizens who have the power of life and death over him. Both this restraint and this silence keep him on the philosopher's course, trying to influence souls through truth-seeking *logos* rather than through wealth or power or mere rhetoric.[167] In the *Phaedrus*, the *daimonion* impels Socrates to recant his first, dreadfully excessive speech (242b8–c3). Here, it playfully holds Socrates within the proper limits of *logos*. The *daimonion* occurs as the strangest sort of impulse, which inspires neither great deeds nor great art, but thoughts of appropriate measure.[168] Thus, the individuality emphasized by Hegel does not concern an inessential individual choice and never concerns anything trivial: *daimonion* is always in service to the calling of philosophy in Socrates.

Thus, the Socratic *daimonion* is a thoughtful transformation of the more full-blown mythical *daimōn*. Like the mythical *daimōn*, the *daimonoi* represented in the dialogues have power, offer guidance, require attention, and animate activity. Throughout the dialogues, a *daimōn* is often likened to a guide. In the *Phaedo*, each newly dead soul is forcibly led away by its appointed *daimōn*. (108b1–3) *Daimōnoi* govern regions in the *Statesman* (274b5–6); each soul chooses one in the *Republic* (617e1). Sometimes they are merely larger and more powerful than mere mortals (*Erōs*, in the *Symposium*, is a great *daimōn*), and they must be honored. There is a right way and a wrong way to speak about them. (*Republic* 392a4–5) They facilitate all exchanges between gods and mortals, as has been noted above. It is not said with any specificity where they come from. The *daimonion* shares the dark origin of the *daimōn* and a general sense of guidance, choice and divine status, but it does not share any of the force, exchange of gifts, leadership, size, or animation of action with its mythical counterpart. By contrast, it stops, restrains and prevents.

But just as the restraining influence of the *daimonion* suggests something different at work than the orientation toward action of a *daimōn*, so also does Socrates' practice of giving a reasoned account (*logos*) soon after the *daimonion* appears. Far from functioning as an authority or a bestower of benefits and/or commands, the *daimonion* induces puzzlement in Socrates, who always questions the reason for this restraint and seeks to discover its appropriateness. In the *Phaedrus*, he accounts for the *daimonion*'s restraining him from crossing the stream and thus from leaving his friend's presence in terms of his having spoken excessively and disgracefully about *Erōs*[169] (242b8–d2); in the *Apology*, the absence of *daimonion* permits Socrates to reflect upon and to speak about that ultimate limit called death as something good.[170] (40a9–c2) Even in the *Euthydemus*, where the advent of the *daimonion* seems most serendipidously prophetic (272e3–273a3), the issue is a discussion of refutation in *logos* which culminates in an exhortation to Crito to examine all things according to the measure of goodness and badness, including philosophy.

In this way, the *mythos* out of which *daimonion* is born provokes investigatory *logos*. In his encounter with the *daimonion* here as elsewhere, the philosophical activity of Socrates makes itself manifest in the interplay of *mythos* and *logos*. *Mythos* is not secondary to *logos* here any more than it is in the realm of the city. Just as in the *Phaedrus*, where Socrates refuses to rationalize the myths since the task of self-knowledge takes all his time (see the previous chapter), *mythos* and the task of self-knowledge are allowed to belong together here as well.

Thus, the voice that restrains together with a reasoned account for that restraint constitute a juncture of *mythos* and *logos* where philosophy can take place. In this light, *daimonion* is no guide or genius, as it seemed to be in the overarching *mythos* about *daimon*. It does not lead Socrates to any action, does not guide his life in any way by itself. *Daimonion* surfaces occasionally but always powerfully, and its power is measured from its alliance with *logos*. The alleged peculiarity of the *daimonion* to Socrates occurs as a special instinct with respect to limits, a gift of strange silent *mythos* which surfaces at the approach to those limits. But its significance is universal. While this gift confers no special moral or epistemological status upon Socrates, the *logoi* disclosed with its aid provide insight which provides guidance for all. So the issue is no specific instance of the welling up of *daimonion* nor is it *daimonion* itself, but the conjunction of *daimonion* and *logos*.

Hegel went wrong locating the *daimonion* between external oracles and mind (together with conscience). It simply cannot be placed anywhere within such a scheme. Further, the charge of peculiarity to Socrates misses the point that for any gift (just as for anything derived from any source) to have philosophical significance, it must be conjoined with *logos*. Yet an odd disjunctive parallel has emerged between conscience (*Gewissen*) and *daimonion*, one based not merely upon their general similarity as directive inner voices: as conscience is allied with knowing and science, *daimonion* is allied with not-knowing and the *mythos* which erupts where science can not enter. The dialogical responses to the *daimonion* occur not as definitive explanations but as thoughtful interpretations which are always open to further questioning. Thus what we might call the conscience-like phenomenon of the Platonic dialogues is much more playful than the ever-serious conscience, looking inward to philosophical life as gentle prod rather than as stern judge.

* *

Nothing like the Socratic *daimonion* occurs in Hegel's modern view of conscience as a faculty belonging to an ethics based on reason, but nothing like the *daimonion* occurs in Aristotle's ethics either. One can see why: while such an ethics is concerned with fixing the principles or faculties or criteria of right action and so eliminating randomness, the *daimonion* makes its appearance as an impulse which occurs more or less randomly. The constraints of law and custom never constrain the *daimonion*. Although it has an influence upon action, its randomness and darkness of origin almost make it seem to be an unruly, anti-ethical presence.

Again, however, this randomness and darkness are allied with rule and order. In other settings than the ones we have already treated, the *daimonion* shows itself as a measuring influence across an expanse reaching beyond the individual soul. The three different occurrences cited below, drawn from later and supposedly more technical dialogues, expose this wider measuring dimension. In the context of the individual soul, we saw *daimonion* marking a certain region beyond the customarily human and between the human and the divine. The mythically inspired constraint upon speech and action placed upon the soul of Socrates by the *daimonion* in the "earlier" dialogues is extended into an inspired measuring of the human world in these "later" passages.

Theaetetus:

> Socrates: "When they come back and beg for a renewal of our association (*sunousia*) with amazing protestations, sometimes the *daimonion* that comes to me forbids it; with others it is permitted; and these begin to make progress. (151a2–5)

Sophist:

> Stranger: Each of these [products of divine workmanship] are followed closely by images (*eidōla*), and these were contrived by daimonic means (*daimonia*)." (266b6–7)

Statesman:

> Stranger: Whenever a true opinion of the beautiful and the just and also the good and the others arises in the souls with the greatest forcefulness, I say it is born in the *daimonion* of a divine people.
>
> Young Socrates: You have spoken appropriately. (309c5–9)

While the *daimonion* in the *Theaetetus* passage fits the pattern of permission/restraint presented thus far, its links with Socrates' midwifery suggest something else as well. Artemis, goddess of midwifery, cannot give birth; midwives can no longer give birth, but have had children in the past "because human nature is too weak to acquire skill when inexperienced." (149c1–2) There are no children of Socrates' soul, but he is able to discern who is pregnant with "a fruitful and true thought" (*hē dianoia ē gonimon te kai alēthes*) (150c2–3). Though he produces and teaches nothing and his patients all learn what they learn from within themselves, "the cause of the delivery is the god and I." (150d9–e1) In every part of the account, human nature is regioned off into exclusive parts: midwifery/giving birth; female (children of body)/male (children of soul); pregnant/barren; divine/human; finally, deserving/undeserving of a second chance with Socrates after leaving him too soon.

It is not at all clear what a "fruitful and true thought" might be, as Socrates gives neither an account nor an example. We may suppose it to belong to wisdom (*sophia*). But wisdom is precisely what Socrates lacks; divine necessity constrains him from giving birth to it. But as we see in this dialogue (and elsewhere in other cases), Theaetetus' child falls far short of the midwife's lofty standard. The final exchange with Theaetetus signals that Socrates' interest lies not so much in the "child" (Theaetetus' thought that knowledge is perception through the senses) but in its parent (Theaetetus himself). As a result of Socrates' art, Theaetetus will either give a better birth in the future upon the basis of the midwife's critique or will be humbler "not supposing you know what you do not know." (210c3–4)

In this light, the *daimonion* spoken of in the *Theaetetus*, which directs Socrates not to permit certain people a second chance after they have left in an untimely fashion, is an outward extension of Socrates' inwardly self-reflective *daimonion*. Just as midwives have had experience with the birth(s) of their own children of the body, Socrates has had much experience with *logoi*, his children of the soul. He can tell by his experience, guided by a well-honed instinct, which potential "new births" do not deserve encouragement.

"The god and I" are the dual cause of what does *not* get fully born: *wisdom*. Not only are there no instances of wise thoughts offered in the *Theaetetus*, not a single "fruitful and true thought" along any of the lines that might be suggested by the context of these words is ever claimed in the entire Platonic corpus. In the face of this lack, "the god and I" are the guarantors of the properly human comportment: *philosophy*. The Socratic *daimonion* is aligned with the god on the side of the prevention of excess in human *logos* (supposing that one knows what one doesn't); Socrates' elenctic activity does kindred work on the side of the actual thoughts. In the *Theaetetus*, the *daimonion* occurs as inspired measuring of the realm of human *logos*, an extension of its restraining function beyond the self-measuring of the individual soul.

The daimonic contrivance of images of divine "originals" in the *Sophist* (e.g. "ourselves, all other living things, the elements of natural things. . .and their offspring" [266b2–4]) is exemplified

> by images in sleep, and in daylight all those self-lit images (*eidōla*) called shadows when dark patches interrupt the light, or a reflection when the light belonging to the eye meets and coalesces with light belonging to something else on a bright and smooth surface and produces a form (*eidos*) yielding an *aisthēsis* which is the reverse of the ordinary direct view. (266b9–c4)

Contrivance "by daimonic means" (*daimonia*) clearly means indirect contrivance, such that a distance opens up between image and original which must be mediated by something else.

On one level, the mediation is fairly straightforward. Both dream images and reflections can be coordinated with the things of nature which are their originals; all the beholder has to do is wake up and/or perceive the relevant original directly. But in both cases, an illumination which is not mentioned in the divine creation is required, not only so that the images can be properly joined to their originals but also so that the distinction between original and image can be made at all. The stranger's account of the production of originals and the production of images (*auto-* and *eidōlopoietikon*) at 266a8–11 does not mention this daimonic illumination, which must allow for darkness in order for both the comparison and the distinction to take place.

Further, what are here called divine "originals" are not true originals but second-order products. The originally divine is precisely what does not come to sensation (*aisthēsis*). The juncture of product and its image in *aisthēsis*, whether in dreams or in a reverse reflection, is the juncture of two images. With the original absent from *aisthēsis*, the two ways of production yield a play of images.

How, then, are products joined to their images? Or in other words, how are sensible "originals" joined to their sensible "images"? How are images related to other images so that their stratification is discernible within *aisthēsis*? Not by sensible means (this would merely multiply the image play beyond any distinction at all) but by a *daimonic* between, which makes itself manifest in the illumination/darkness which allows for comparison and distinction.

Sallis notes that the *Sophist* provides "more than sufficient occasion to wonder whether the method of collection and division. . .is not, in the end, incapable of distinguishing between the philosopher and the sophist."[171] To be sure, the daimonic in the *Sophist* occurs as internal to an image-making process which is presented as unproblematically accomplished by a god. But its presence between products and their images (or between sensible originals and their images) points to a split within *aisthēsis* which resonates throughout the dialogues on all their levels. The split animates the puzzle of "image" and "original," and the ongoing issues which are played out in its terms, most notably the distinction between the philosopher and the sophist. This distinction does not come clearly to *logos* in the dialogue, although it is intimated in a way that might be called "daimonic." No knowledge is claimed.

In accord with this aporetic outcome, "true opinion" (*alēthē doxan*) and "greatest forcefulness" (*bebaiōseōs*) are the key words of the proclamation of the stranger in the *Statesman* (cited above) concerning the beautiful, the just and the good in relation to the daimonic. The young Socrates calls these words "appropriate" (*prepei*). These true opinions, which enter and fill the soul with force, serve to restrain a people by instilling moderation and prudence.

Forged by the statesman's "music (*mousē*) of the art of kingship" (309d2–3), these qualities spread themselves through a population and fashion the individual into a "willing member of a community of the just." (309e1–2) The inspiration of the statesman is extended through the daimonic capacity of the people by means of his education of them. The forcefulness with which the qualities enter and remain in the souls of men signals its extension of an individual gift across a wide expanse. The extension of the statesman's divine gift through nurture of his subjects harmonizes the two types of citizens, the courageous and the moderate, who would otherwise be at odds. (310a1–5)

There is a strong sense in which this account in the *Statesman* would be well-placed in Chapter 8 on comedy. For the passage on the divinely inspired education of the *daimonion* of a people occurs between two passages which would seem to be at strong odds with it. In the preceding passage (309e10–14) the statesman's art is likened to weaving, with the king as master weaver having strict control over his subjects and combining them into a community. However, he does not accomplish this union by weaving or by any other art. Rather, he requires the aforementioned divine shaping of the *daimonion*, which is not under the control of the art of weaving (or any other art) at all. The subsequent passage (310a7–b5) insists upon the statesman's need and right to supervise marriages so that the brave and the moderate are mixed for the good of the community. This assumes a daimonic control of the erotic by human means. However, the erotic is itself daimonic (cf. *Symposium*) and impossible to bring under control by any human art.[172]

The use of *daimonion* in the *Statesman* seems to depart dramatically from its employment in the earlier dialogues. A certain collection of definite opinions are dumped into a people's *daimonion*, and there seems to be no room for the questioning and the playfulness associated with its Socratic analogue. Together with its uses in the other later dialogues, it seems less aligned with its reflection-provoking significance for the individual soul than with the extension of a measuring influence through prominent young men (*Theaetetus*), through the entire world of "things" and their "images" (*Sophist*), and through the political world (*Statesman*).

But in all cases the betweenness of *daimonion* is affirmed, together with its measuring. The midwife exposed the misbegotten child, but declares that artist's willingness to attempt another birth when the *daimonion* does not prevent his going forward. Daimonic contrivance in the *Sophist* exposed the image-play of all *aisthēsis*, together with the need for illumination by a source beyond this play located between gods and mortals. And the weaver-king in the *Statesman* required access both to the Muses and to the *daimonion* of his people in order to perform his art (of instilling true opinions, not knowledge) with the proper measure.

Ultimately, the *daimonion* provides directedness toward measure but no real content. Even in the case of the *Statesman*, the dumped-in opinions seem to be nothing more than inspired praises of courage, moderation and their mutual tolerance. To say that the inspired statesman instills them in the *daimonion* indicates nothing more than its receptivity to divine sources. The same can be said of its earlier, Socratic manifestation, although in the later dialogues the questioning self-reflection provoked by the *daimonion* recedes.

The *daimonion* provides a fruitful entrance to the play of the Platonic dialogues. By itself it is virtually mute and arrives out of the dark, indicating to Socrates only that restraint might be wise on his current course. The space made open by the *daimonion* between god and mortals, beyond the customarily human, is therefore a space within which proper measure may be sought. In the act of entering this space, the *daimonion* of Socrates discloses it in its playful character. The comedy of an instinct which restrains and of a dark flash giving birth to the light of *logos* is reflected in the counterimage of tragedy, the danger of *hubris* against which the *daimonion* at play guards by provoking mindfulness of proper measure. In connection with *logos*, the *daimonion* can open a space for a wisdom-seeking soul, a well-designed city, an understood world—and hold each so that the limits of human insight are not transgressed. Because darkness as well as light will always belong to the juncture of *daimonion* and *logos*, play will always belong to its products as well.

CHAPTER ELEVEN:
MIMĒSIS AT PLAY

Mimēsis (imitation) can be approached most fruitfully not in terms of a theory of art but as another prominent phenomenon within the play of the Platonic dialogues. Like discussions of writing and occurrences of *daimonion*, the issue of *mimēsis* surfaces only occasionally in the dialogues but shapes them profoundly. The dialogues are self-reflectively written. They are informed by inspiration. Also, they are imitations.

Regarded in this way, the famous passage near the beginning of Book X resonates beyond the immediate context of the threefold denigration of Homer:

> Then it looks like we're pretty well agreed on these things: (1) the imitator knows (*eidenai*) nothing worth mentioning about what he imitates; (2) imitation is a kind of play and not serious and (3) those who take up tragic poetry in iambic and epics are all imitators in the highest possible degree. (602b6–10) [numbering is mine]

These three positions upon which Socrates and Glaucon are "pretty well agreed" sound damning. But upon more careful inspection, all three admit of an equally friendly interpretation. Regarding (1), we have seen on many occasions that poetic imitation proceeds by inspiration and not knowledge. It is also clear from the *Apology* and the *Theaetetus* that the ignorance ascribed to the imitators could also be ascribed to Socrates. In the former, Socrates says that the poets proceed from inspiration and enthusiasm and don't know what they say, though much of it is fine (*kala*)(22c1–3)[173]; in the latter, Socrates as midwife does not give birth to any wisdom. (150c3–7) The connection made between imitation and ignorance in (1) could indeed be heard as a denigration of imitators as people who, acting from ignorance but with selfish design, attempt to influence others through the skillful manipulation of imagery. But this connection can also be heard playfully, as binding philosophers as well as poets to the non-rational, inspired and therefore non-knowledge-giving sources which they require as a result of the ignorance to which they are given over by nature.

(2) can be heard as saying that imitation is entirely frivolous, and therefore does not deserve serious attention. According to this perspective, the treatment of imitation in the Platonic dialogues has the overcoming of its charms through knowledge as its goal. But calling imitation "playful and not serious" can also be heard playfully, and with a playfulness in full accord with the rigors of the Platonic texts. As we have seen, play in the *Republic* is called the first entry into education, and seriousness without play begets inappropriate transgression.[174] In the *Laws*, this initiating educational play has no serious correlate, but is associated only with the delight taken in the gracefulness of music (*charitos*).[175] (667e2–8) In (2), play without seriousness seems to be an entirely blameworthy quality. But heard playfully, this pure playfulness is the best entrance into education for the human soul. In this light, the assertion in (2) that imitators are playful and not serious can be heard as praise.

In (3), poets are called imitators in the highest degree. The many "fine" (*kala*) things said by the poets according to Socrates (once again, see *Apology* 22c3) testifies to his acknowledgement of the worthy serious content within poetry's play. Insofar as mere play serves as the entry to education and insofar as the content of poetic imitation as example of this mere play can be fine (*kala*), (3) admits to a reverse reading. Calling poets imitators to the highest degree may be damning them as third from truth, but it may just as well be praising them for their contribution to the education of the soul.

Like writing, which was itself seen as an image (*eidotos*) of speaking (*Phaedrus* 276a8–9) and which could either remind one of something known but forgotten in the soul or promote laziness and forgetfulness in it, *mimēsis* is presented in a double aspect. The activities (i.e. writing, imitation) appear positively at some places in the dialogues and negatively at others, depending upon which aspect is highlighted in the discussion and which recedes from view. This double aspect has already been adumbrated in Chapter 7, where it was shown how Homer's "Achilles in Hades" passage was censored and then resuscitated. Because it would inspire fear of death in the guardians, it was excised from their education (387b8ff); because it would inspire the one who left the cave with the courage to dwell nearer to what is true and farther from what is shadowy, it was brought back. (516d4–7) On one side is the unreflective beholding of what is presented, so that the image or imitation is thoughtlessly regarded as if it were original and authoritative. On the other is a reflective beholding, in which the images are at play with originals on another level and can transport the beholder to another perspective.

The double aspect is presented more generally (and playfully) at the beginning of Book X: "[poetic imitations] seem to maim the thought of those who hear them and do not have knowledge (*to eidenai*) of how they really are as a *pharmakon*." (595b5–7) Again, there is no declaration of harm on the unreflective side, only of "seeming" harm. On the reflective side, one can protect oneself from whatever harm imitations cause merely by knowing what they are. This knowledge is the elixir for the illness of having the (internal or external) city ruled by the kind of pleasure and pain produced by poetic imitations, rather than ruled by law and the best *logos*. (607a6–8)

At least as much here as elsewhere, attention to the playfulness of the dialogues is necessary for a proper interpretation of a crucial issue encountered in them. Failure to take it into account has led to widespread blundering on the matter of *mimēsis*, in which Plato has been ascribed views which the text exposes as partial at best and ultimately insupportable. For example, Plato has been said to despise or at least to distrust art, and to hold a theory of forms along the lines of a metaphysical realism. The discussion of the couch-imitation in Book X of the *Republic* addresses both of these. It opens out into the apparent denigration of imitators and to the relegation of poetry to its "third from truth" status, according to which it waters the basest part of the soul and serves as the enemy of those qualities a city should most wish to nurture. And it appears to proclaim that the forms (*eidē*) have real being while its imitations have something less. But this discussion also and at once moves in another way, toward other outcomes.

The movement of the argument seems straightforward, from original to image (imitation) to more distant image (*eidōlon*). The *eidos* of couch (which *is* in nature) is one; the craftsman makes many couches according to this one *eidos*; the imitator imitates an aspect of the look of one or more of the crafted couches. But there are peculiarities in the design of the discussion, which reveal inner tensions and anomalies. These aspects of the discussion's play disclose the genuine Platonic outlook on imitation.

Triad 1	*Triad 2*	*Triad 3*
a god	*eidos* of couch	*eidos* of couch in nature
craftsman	couch	*eidos* of actual couches
painter	couch-imitation	*eidos* of imitated couches

The matter seems to turn upon the exploitation of a straightforward original-image relation. Triad 2, the "*eidos* of couch/ couch/ couch-imitation" triad, has a parallel triad of "god/ couchmaker (i.e. craftsman)/painter of couch" (Triad 1). But the latter triad of producers "preside[s] over three *eidē* of couches" (Triad 3)! (597b13–14) Even the loosest translation of *eidos* in Triad 3 (e.g. as "kind" of couch) disrupts the relation of producer to production illustrated by the parallelism of triads 1 and 2. Triad 3 claims that the craftsman fashions the couch in accord with an *eidos* peculiar to his human realm, rather than that of the god as claimed in Triad 1. Further, the painter-imitator, earlier said to orient himself according neither to the one couch in nature nor to the actuality of the craftsman's couch but only according to its "appearing as it appears" (598a3–4), is now said to produce according to an *eidos* peculiar to imitated couches. Thus, the imitator in Triad 3 is accorded a reflectiveness denied him in Triad 2, making him no longer a mere copier.

Further disrupting the account from within is the parallelism itself. Triad 1 and Triad 2 relate to one another as original and image, as producer and produced. But the image-original relation is precisely what the discussion of imitation is at pains to exhibit. To this circularity at the source of the schema, Triad 3 adds an inner incoherence. Triad 3, which contains *eidē* over which Triad 1 is said to have authority (597b13), is regarded to be determinative itself in Triad 1: the *eidos* (and the god) preside over the two below in Triads 1 and 2, but the two below preside over *eidē* in Triad 3.

When we move upward within the triads and approach the top, we discover a dramatic recoil similar to the one that is discovered when we ascend the divided line. In both cases, the *eidē* which would account for everything else are not fully present. By its own measure (as mathematical), the divided line itself is no better than one below the top level of *eidē*, and perhaps belongs at the lowest rung (as an image). Moving to the triads, in Triads 1 and 2 (ignoring the complication introduced by Triad 3), on the bottom level both producer and produced occur in the realm of the visible, with the painting serving as the "image" of the visible "original" thing. By contrast, on the middle level the craftsman works across the divide of visible and intelligible, consulting the *eidos* in order to fashion the "thing." But on the highest level of the *eidos*, neither the producer nor the mode of production are clearly present at all. On the level where things are supposed to be clearest and most certain, the dialogue reads:

> . . .[The couch] that is in nature,. . .*we would say, I suppose* (*hēn phaimen an, hos egōmai*) a god produced. Or who else?
> No one else, I suppose. (597b5–9; emphasis mine)

Thus the gods, the ultimate producers of the *eidē* which drive the entire discussion of imitation, are present only by supposition, i.e. by a certain opinion. On the level of the craftsman's art this is not much of an issue, since only the *eidos* and the *technē* are necessary for its performance. But the absence of the producer at the top dramatically affects the "producers" at the "bottom," the so-called imitators. For the poets are said to be imitators to the highest degree, so it would seem that their work would occur as mere copies of visible things, either crafted or natural. But they clearly are not.[176] On the contrary, the gods which are present only by "supposition" in the philosophical discussion of the *eidē* acquire a fuller and more powerful presence in poetry. The lack of full presence of the god in the account of production and imitation images the lack of full presence of the *eidē* in the account of knowledge, just as the tangles in each indicate an ascent and descent riddled with obstructions.

The relation in philosophical argument of the gods to real being and its imitations was also treated in the *Cratylus* and the *Sophist*. A brief detour in their direction will be taken before returning to the philosophical celebration of Homeric poetry and its transformation of the understanding of *mimēsis* in the *Republic*.

In the *Cratylus*, where the issue occurs in terms of naming, Socrates and Cratylus agree that a name is an imitation of the being (*ousia*) of each thing imitated. (421c12–424b2) The primary or first (*prōta*) names are the irreducible ones which prevent an endless regress in *logos*; a primary name is bound to the thing named so that the name is, in truth, its imitation. The difficulty resides in the inaccessibility of the primary names. But these names are precisely what the discussion demands in order to deliver upon its promise of accounting for the original fashioning of names in accord with the being of things! After suggesting a "re-enactment" of the ancient way of name-making through the division and subdivision of the letters (of words) into classes and subclasses so that a scientific view (*epistēsometha skopeisthai*) can be obtained, Socrates playfully throws up his hands and says:

> Shall we leave [the primary names], or shall we attempt to learn what little is within our power, saying in advance as I said before of the gods, that we know

(*eidotes*) nothing about the truth of them but we imagine (*eikazomen*) opinions (*dogmata*) of them. . . (425b8–c2)

What follows is the same recourse to the strongest, healthiest *logos* that has been mentioned earlier[177] and will be discussed in the final chapter in connection with the argument for the immortality of the soul. No claim is made that the premises are true, but only that there are none as strong as the ones offered. The "doctrine" of the imitation of objects in names is not based upon knowledge as noetic insight into being, but upon its being the outcome of the strongest argument upon the subject that human power can fashion. Socrates says that any sort of ignorance of the primary names involves ignorance of secondary words (426a3–5), so it is guaranteed that some sort of ignorance dwells at the heart of the account.

There is no need here to argue either the merits or the ultimate "seriousness" of Socrates' earlier derivation of the divine names from the human things which they govern. It is enough to note a basic similarity between that exercise and the "scientific" division and collection of the letters into classes (*eidē*) and subclasses: in both cases, the activity of naming has already taken place, and the original/imitation relation essential to it has already been constituted in advance of the discussion of naming as original/imitation relation. Thus, both the admission of ignorance regarding the primary names and the circularity of the efforts to account for the nature of imitation indicate the problematic manner in which this discussion takes place.

At 426a2, Socrates speaks of two recourses ("elegant excuses"—"*ekduseis . . .kompsai*"): (1) to the very old age and barbarous origin of the primary names; (2) to the gods, after the manner of tragic poets. However, both recourses are generated not by imitation at all, but by extension of the surrounding *logos*. In the first case the account extends backward to a time before our awareness, and in the second it extends to an originary realm beyond our ability to see and understand. These two (especially the latter) are neither merely imagined nor dispensable, but constitute an important part of the realm we inhabit, serving as measuring limits in terms of time and of origin. They are places we can surely imagine but just as surely cannot visit. Taking recourse to the gods in the manner of tragic poets is dismissed playfully:

> . . .like the tragic poets, who in any perplexity have their gods waiting in the air,
> . . .we must get out of our difficulty by saying that 'the gods gave the first names and they are right'. . . (425d5–d9)

But the seriousness underlying the play is the inability to account for the naming/named relation as a relation of the being of a thing to its imitation in human *logos*. Of course this is a caricature of the treatment of the gods by the tragic poets, but it is a playfully accurate treatment of human beings trying to account for original naming. In the *Timaeus*, for example, the speaker issues a "call upon god. . .to be our savior from a strange (*atopou*) and unaccustomed (*aēthous*) inquiry, and to bring us to the haven of likely opinion (*eikotōn dogma*)" (48d4–5); only then does he declare the visible to be the imitation (*mimēma*) of the intelligible patterns (48e4–7). These patterns enter and leave the (already unaccountable and wondrous) receptacle by a process he calls "unaccountable and wondrous." (*dusphraston*; *thaumaston*—50c6) However, there is a "between," a healthiest human *logos* which may escape the interlocutors of the *Cratylus*, and which avoids the radical skepticism which seems entailed by the absence of fixed names. It would account for the naming process as we know it, however much it may fall short of that originary knowledge of the relation of the gods to being which would complete the account of imitation[178].

Thus, imitation with regard to names takes place playfully, in a realm which is both sectioned off and shaped by what is withheld from it. Given the ignorance of primary names and the mythical extension of the realm under the sway of our *logos* to account for it, the imitation process itself is a function of the same image-play it would escape and for which it would at least partially account. Imitation, then, is not primarily the name of a relation between original and image such that the latter accurately copies the former. Rather, the mimetic is itself an image of that play whereby human seeing and knowing, blocked off from ultimates it can discern but never truly know, seeks to understand, judge and enjoy what it is given.

At 235a1 in the *Sophist*, the Stranger calls his quarry "clearly a wizard, an imitator of beings (*mimētēs ōn tōn ontōn*)," and in its final pages the Stranger culminates the division/collection process with a discussion of imitation, understood as a "kind of production (*poiēsis*), though only of images, as we say, but not of each thing itself." (265b1–2) He then divides production into divine and human, then subdivides each into originals and images in this way (there are further divisions, but these are enough for our purposes):

PRODUCTION

	original	image
DIVINE	original	image
HUMAN	original	image

Even leaving out of account any questions one might have about the suitability of the division/collection process,[179] there is another disruption of apparent symmetry and order from within. Divine originals comprise the things of nature. Their images, as we have seen in the previous chapter, are dream images, shadows and distorted perceptions of things which occur in disturbances of light. Human originals consist of made things such as houses, while the house in a painting fashioned by a painter is its corresponding human image. One dimension is missing from the discussion: only visible things count as originals, and so the *eidos* or being in accord with which they are produced and which is essential to any act of imitation is absent!

At that crucial point where the sophist is to be identified by the nature of his imitation (ignorant vs. knowing), the Stranger seems to grasp the difficulty. (267d1–2) He admits to not knowing imitation's right names and. . .blames the ancients for being lazy "with regard to the division of kinds (*genōn*) according to forms (*eidē*)[!]" (267d5–6; exclamation mine) Thus the "daring" names he gives ("supposed mimicry" (*doxomimētikēn*) and "learned mimicry" (*historikēn. . .mimēsin* [267e1–2]) have no rooting in divine production which would assure the appropriateness of the imitation. Their source is found in the human realm, and enacted after the manner of the painter who is far removed from the divine original. Both kinds of mimicry are imitations of and in the human realm, and so can hardly account for the distinction between philosophical and sophistic imitation.

So divine production, never very clear, is absent from the task for which it was most needed in the dialogue, the distinguishing of the sophist from others who may resemble him. But again, this absence opens up the play-space of the dialogue and of the human *logos* it enacts, allowing both sophistry and philosophy to come forth. It grants the playground upon which both human ignorance and human efforts to exploit or remedy it encounter one another, perhaps in battle. This playground may be "bigger" (a city) or "smaller" (an individual soul). Imitation of an intelligible or a divine original may clearly occur, but is never accountable by argument. The field upon which the issue of imitation occurs is shot through with ignorance and darkness. A full-blown theory accounting for the key features of imitation in human life would require a field of transparency to which we have no access.

The nature of this playground suggests that the issue may be less one of forming a theory of imitation than of playfully locating, questioning, interpreting and enjoying imitations within the human search for wisdom.

* *

The works of Homer, the tragic poets and the other imitators are said to have the capacity to maim those who lack knowledge of what they are as a remedy. But of what does this healing knowledge consist? It seems to involve nothing more than the awareness that the poems are imitations and not originals. There is a distance between the poems and the soul that hears them, and between the poems and the matters of which they sing. The double aspect of the "third from truth" discussion shows that while the poems can be seen as images of things and more distant images of the *eidē*, they are also detached and detachable from their constraints. The positive significance of the distance of the poems from the truth of the *eidē* of objects is that they are creations (not direct representations), and so offer vicarious participation of the soul in important human matters (not merely copies for comparison with their originals).

Our detour pointed out the impossibility of a full account of imitation, and the snares awaiting the attempt. But no deep understanding of *mimēsis* is required, nor would such an understanding add much to the experience of poetry. Who has ever mistaken an actual couch for the *eidos* of a couch "which we would say, I suppose, a god produced?" (597b6–7) Who has ever had perception so maimed by a skillful imitator that he actually tried to recline upon a painting of a couch? The optical illusion Socrates proposes at 598b9–c4 could deceive only children and foolish human beings, and even they would eventually detect it.

And who has ever mistaken a poetic phrase for its "original," *Eōs krokopeplos* ("yellow-robed dawn") for an actual dawning? Even Socrates' claim that "all except for a very rare few" (605c6–7) are maimed must be taken playfully. Socrates implicitly confesses to his joining "even the best of us" (605c10) who "enjoy it and. . .give ourselves over to following the imitation; suffering along with the hero in all seriousness. . ." But no one is maimed. Even in this intense vicarious participation, there is no mistaking of oneself for the hero, or the hero for a real colleague. A very rare few may be able to resist the power of the imagery, but his words and actions on this matter suggest that the inability to resist hardly seems dangerous to the health of the soul in the rest of us, including Socrates.

But if virtually everyone has this precious knowledge which liberates one from the soul-maiming threatened by poetic imitation, what is the issue? Great poetry is itself a *pharmakon* which induces forgetfulness of this protective distance. As we have seen, the would-be guardian is defenseless against its power, and so must not hear Achilles' lament from Hades; it might maim his soul, which is identified completely with his function in the city. But the one who has been liberated from the shadows is capable of reflection and the distance opened by it. This liberation consists precisely in the ability to distinguish shadows from the things of which they are shadows. So unlike the would-be guardian, his soul can defend itself from the danger of unreflective identification. He can encounter the poem at a protective distance from his soul, and can thus hear the words of Achilles' lament as a celebration of a certain kind of life, interpreting Hades as the realm of shadows and the earth above as nearer to truth. But in the powerful vicarious participation there is always the possibility of a forgetfulness which erases that distance.[180] This closing of the distance is the essence of the maiming; it can close off the self-reflectiveness required for the capacity to choose well (with all that this implies) which marks our humanity. The forgetfulness of distance can lead to forgetfulness of the proper limits of the human world. *Hubris* is always a danger for a human being.

Thus, to the question of how to banish the possibility of an excessive and/or inappropriate response to a poetic imitation, there is no answer. The possibility of an inappropriate, perhaps damaging response is always alive. But the price of banishing the great and provocative works of art from any society in speech or in actuality (as if it were possible) is the deprivation of nourishment that the human soul needs. Great poetry serves the soul as it challenges it, shows the soul its possible liberation even as it may endanger it.

Knowledge of "how poetic imitations truly are" does not imply mastery or control or even suppression of the effect of powerful poetical images which would otherwise maim the soul. Socrates calls this knowledge a *pharmakon,*[181] which retains its manifold sense of drug, transporter, bewitcher, remedy, etc.[182] Every bit as much as the beautiful images in Homer charm the soul, luring it away from everyday concerns and into the sublime realm of the poem, philosophical thoughts (e.g. of the *eidē*, of justice) elicit an ascent of the soul from the usual concerns to a city which may exist only in *logos*. And just as the journey of the soul inspired by poetry can lead to excess through a dominance of pleasure and pain, so too can the journey inspired by philosophy lead to excess, e.g. through the various corruptions spoken of in Book VI. (490e2–497a8)

Thus, when philosophy encounters poetry in Book X, imitation encounters imitation, enchantment encounters enchantment. It is not a contest of austere knowledge vs. a charming, manipulative ignorance, nor is it a contest between the power of reason and the power of emotion. They really are at odds, and their difference shows itself in reciprocal accusations of excess, issuing from the lack of reasoned account in poetry, and from the pretentiousness to wisdom in philosophy. (See Chapter 8) They share, however, a common source.

In what sense are the *dialogues* imitations? In one sense, they are imitations of original *logoi* of some kind (perhaps of real conversations, perhaps of conversations in the mind of their author, perhaps both, etc.) In another, they can be seen as imitations which seek to participate in those originals about which they frequently speak, called *eidē* in the dialogues. We have seen throughout that the *eidē*, the most important originals of all, are not fully present. That is, they are present in thought, serving as a way of fixing attention (*apoblepsis*) (*Parmenides* 135b7); they are hypothesized as touchstones of truth (*Phaedo* 100b5–8); they are interpreted as the invisible, intelligible structure of the visible world. But an essential measure of absence belongs to them: they are never present in themselves, through themselves.

The most important goal of the dialogues, wisdom, is also present as absent. The interpenetration of this presence and absence occurs most dramatically in Socrates' awareness of his own ignorance, but also in his aporetic encounters with various sophists and their pupils (e.g. *Laches*, *Gorgias*, *Protagoras*, *Meno*) and in dialogues culminating in myths (*Republic*, *Timaeus*) which bear implicit witness to this ignorance.

So the dialogues show that neither their ultimate objects of knowledge nor their ultimate goal is available within them. Nor is any means suggested which would lead one directly from the imitations of knowledge and wisdom to the originals which they imitate. The only recourse one has to those crucial originals which provide orientation is indirect, through their manifestation in and to human *logos*. Socrates says that imitation "is surely far from the truth. . .because it lays hold of a certain small part of each thing, and that part is itself only a more distant image (*eidōlon*)." (598b6–8) On this basis, the dialogues are imitations and so belong to the same class as the distant image (*eidōlon*) of the carpenter painted by someone who knows little or nothing of the art of carpentry. (598b8–c4) But given the missing originals on the level of intellect and their muteness and concealedness in the realm of visible things, these imitations provide the best access we have to them. The space they leave open allows for the activity whereby humans can attain their due measure of insight and wisdom.

What about this absence and concealment, and these defects issuing from them? How crucial are such considerations to the dialogues, and to the poems they contend with? *This absence is precisely why there are poems and dialogues at all*! The mythical realm of the gods is the counterpart of the philosopher's absent originals in the dialogues. The accompanying lack of insight into originals and ultimates in the human arena is precisely what calls poetry and philosophy forth, together with their dangers and their possibilities of transcendence.

This is why they are contenders in the soul and for the soul in the Platonic dialogues, which are philosophical dialogues where strains of the poetic realm surface powerfully. This is why Socrates does not suggest exerting the power of *logos* as reason in order to master the poetic, but rather urges the chanting of *logoi* as countercharm to the charm of poetry.[183] This is why the *Gorgias* ends with a myth drawing upon Homeric images.[184] (523a1–527e7) And this is why the *Republic*, so often cited as an enemy of Homer and of the poetic, concludes with a philosophical imitation of a poetic (and Homeric) imitation which incorporates both philosophical and poetic imitations, and which presents the philosophic life in a beautiful poetical image—the myth of Er.

Great pleasure, as well, is taken in the philosophical life. If there is one steady feature throughout the Socratic dialogues (and I would say, through the others as well, though in a different mode), cheerfulness is it. The dialogical process discloses, as akin to the recognition of ignorance and the search for the good, ongoing delight taken in the mere activity of philosophical thought. *Mimēsis* also provides occasion for this pleasure.

What about pleasure, imitation and philosophical activity? The *Philebus* places pleasure well below measure, beauty, and *nous*, though room is left for "painless pleasures of the soul itself, some attaching to knowledge, others to sensation." (66c4–6) Poetry mediated by the knowledge of its nature as a *pharmakon*, thus freed from its capacity to harm the soul, would surely seem to qualify as such a pleasure. In the *Republic*, desire for pleasure is clearly placed as the lowest of the three parts of the soul, but it is a part that must be fed for the soul to function as it should. Imitation is a component of this diet.

Also in the *Republic*, Socrates often speaks of the pleasure and delight taken in imitations, a pleasure which one cannot shake off and which only philosophical self-reflection can properly measure, and which therefore cannot be excised but must be incorporated into the education of the soul. In the *Laws*, imitation is the basis of all necessary preliminary learning, and the learner is taught by his play. Indeed, all pleasures and desires (*hēdonas, epithumias*) are to be directed through playing (*paidion*). (643c3–9) And the end toward which this pleasure is directed is. . .play![185] While there are serious admonitions concerning (for example) the corruption of souls which do not imitate the philosophic nature (*Republic* 490e2ff), they do not vitiate either the pleasure taken in imitation, the soul's need of imitation, nor even the pleasure taken in the measuring of imitation and its pleasure.

CHAPTER TWELVE:
PLAY AND IMMORTALITY

The soul's immortality is treated with the same playfulness as other issues in the dialogues. This is not to say that the arguments are not seriously offered and are not the best that Plato can present, nor that they are disbelieved either by the characters who utter them or by their absent author. But this seriousness is enclosed within that same playfulness that surrounds discussions of the forms (*eidē*), the city and other matters of import. As we will see, death is every bit as much an occasion for cheerfulness as anything else could be. The issue of death is situated not beyond but within the play which governs, otherwise known as philosophical activity. The blissful life, said to await the one who has been freed from the body and its evils, is not cause but consequence of this cheerfulness.

Playfulness in Plato is a philosophical comportment toward those limits which might otherwise discourage, such as the soul's inherent ignorance, its only partial discernment of ultimate originals which might serve as touchstones of truth, and its often foolish orientation toward pleasure. Interpreted within the playfulness of the Platonic dialogues, these limits become enticements for the soul's engagement in pursuits which foster the best possible discharge of its powers. Even the question of the ultimate destiny of human life, "does the soul continue to live a real existence after the body decays?," propels the soul into activities which enlarge and enhance its sense of life and of its own contribution to its destiny. In the case of Socrates, these include the deeds recounted in the *Phaedo*, from the practicing of music to the offering of the hemlock as a libation.

It should be no surprise that the issue of immortality, a matter that is clearly closed off from direct human insight, is unmistakably signalled as playful in all of its appearances in the dialogues. Nor can there be much surprise at the affiliation of the question of immortality with *nous* and the *eidē*, which are closed off from human knowledge in a kindred way. Those matters which are associated with a kind of perfection—flawlessness, complete knowing, goodness itself—are also found aligned with immortality. But the access to immortality, by argument or otherwise, is fatefully conditioned by its bond to what is mortal.

"Haven't you perceived (*ēsthēsthai*) that our soul is immortal and never destroyed?," (608d3–4) Socrates asks a startled Glaucon in Republic X, as though poor Glaucon has somehow overlooked the readily available good news. But sense-perception (*aisthēsis*) is dramatically unsuited for the grasping of immortality, having the opposed tendency of fixing the soul on what is finite and mortal. If *aisthēsis* has a point of departure that is significant for the matter of immortality, it is that immortality "begins" precisely where all *aisthēsis* and all matters of the body leave off! To suppose that the immortality of the soul can be perceived by the senses is preposterous.

Still more outrageously, Socrates invites Glaucon to say that the soul is immortal for the further reason that "it's not hard." (608d8–9) But the easy argument designed to produce the *aisthēsis* of immortality in Glaucon does not rest upon or proceed by *aisthēsis* at all. Rather, this argument (608e6–611a3) takes its departure from the difference between calling something good (saving and benefitting) and calling something bad (dissolving and destroying). Its main premise is that it is impossible for anything bad to introduce a badness of soul into the soul which would destroy it. The argument concludes therefrom to the soul's immortality.

But the "ease" of this argument, already belied by the playful exchange which initiated it, is belied again by what follows it. Apparently, the soul in its immortality was not properly revealed in this argument according to Socrates, who says, "Now we were telling the truth about it as it appears (*phainetai*) at present: but that is based on the state in which we saw it ourselves (*tetheametha*)" (611c6–7); it was not seen "such as it is in truth." (611b10) Thus, the "easy" immortality apprehended through appearance (but grasped through a difficult argument which makes no reference to appearance at all!) turns out to fall short of truth. Even construed apart from the playfulness in which it is situated, Socrates' argument admittedly does not reach the soul's true immortality.

How, then, can one best see the soul in its optimal condition, so that its immortality can be truly beheld? One must look, says Socrates, to. . ."its love of wisdom (*philosophian*)[!]" (611d7–e1; exclamation mine) This means that in order to see the soul's immortality in its truth, one must see the soul (1) in its *lack* of wisdom, in its lack of access to those originary insights and perfect conditions, and (2) together with its love of what is lacking. The love of wisdom which marks the philosopher, the desire to overcome the ignorance and folly to which one is given over and thus to achieve what is best for a human being, is the mark of a mortal being. The wonder upon the face of Glaucon at Socrates' blithe announcement of the soul's immortality (608d5), reminiscent of the wonder which Socrates called the experience (*pathos*) of the philosopher and philosophy's only origin in the *Theaetetus* (155d2–4]), is a fully philosophical response to Socrates' philosophical play. The play is measured and transformed into something closer to earth when Socrates calls philosophy the soul's vantage point from which to behold its immortality on account of its kinship to it.

More particularly, the look toward philosophy returns the conversation to the wages of justice and injustice on the mortal plane, before death. But like the discussion of immortality, the treatment of the wages of justice is comically inadequate, and completely sails over the issues with which the dialogue has wrestled throughout. Without argument, Socrates asserts (and Glaucon agrees) that sooner or later (perhaps after death), the gods will reward the just and punish the unjust. (612b7–613b8) Without transition and again without argument, the two then agree that this apportionment of rewards will come sooner, i.e. in this life, rather then later.

> . . .it's precisely the just, when they get older, who will rule in their city if they wish ruling offices, and marry. . .and give in marriage. . .whomever they want. (613d1–d4)

Socrates makes no attempt to connect the results of Book IV, in which justice is defined as each part of the soul minding its own business, with these rewards bestowed by the city upon such souls. The two seem internally contradictory, since a just artisan would only mind his art, which keeps him far from high office. Nor is anything said about how the philosophical, justice-practicing soul inevitably comes to be offered the rule. Given the virtually certain bypassing of the philosopher for ruling spoken of in Books V-VI, this also looks like an internal contradiction. If these are not contradictory, then some argument is required. But none is offered.

Further, if the passage from 611e1–614a2 presented sound arguments, then all of Books III-IX and their main insights could have been excised. Justice as a kind of self-discipline apart from any civic reward would be discarded. Philosophy as concerned with truth and the good apart from civic reward would not be an issue at all. The inevitable decline of cities and human beings in them by virtue of their injustice would not take place. All would be well, for cities and for human beings, in the not too distant future. One would merely have to await the old age of the just. But this passage is comedy, pure play, abstracting the brightness from the soul's entire journey. It presents the passages through life and from life to death as if they contained only apparent obstructions, which are overcome so long as one philosophizes. But philosophy is necessary precisely because there are real obstacles, both within and without.

The appropriate darkening occurs in the myth of Er. This tale must be seen as a continuation of the celebration of philosophy begun above, since the most important thing that either happens or does not happen to an individual soul concerns its relation to philosophy. Even in Hades, the soul philosophizes. So even if all of the arguments for the soul's immortality were sound, its immortality would make no essential difference to it. The soul would still be presented with choices of better and worse and it would still have to philosophize in order to choose in the best way.

But even if all of the arguments for the immortality of the soul were bad arguments, it would still make no essential difference to the soul. In order to choose what is best among the options, wherever these choices were offered and whatever they were, the soul would still have to philosophize. What, in this light, can one say about Glaucon's and Adiemantus' concern for the rewards of justice? Given Socrates' transparently comic attribution of eventual civic honors to the just when they get old, and the mythical and unverifiable attribution of "good lives" to them after they die, we are thoroughly ignorant of the rewards for justice.[186] A philosophical stance toward the wages of justice requires, therefore, that they not be taken very seriously.

The myth of Er is supposed to tell the fate of souls after death and before their (re)birth and so to illuminate the proper comportment of souls in relation to their embodiment. However, it turns out that the same crucial piece of information is missing to the strong Er that mortals on earth also lack:

> However, in what way and how he came into his body, he did not know; but, all of a sudden, he recovered his sight and saw that it was morning and he was lying on the pyre. (621b5–7)

The tale which would illuminate the immortal soul's fate after death culminates in a sudden and inexplicable re-thrusting back into mortality and the realm of sight. The reborn Er is given over to the telling of dreamlike myths which raise the very same questions (and locate the teller within the very same darkness) which first give rise to *mythos*. The reborn Er, then, is just like the earlier Er in this regard: mortal, forgetful, given over to *aisthēsis*.[187] But having undergone the powerful education of the journey to Hades presented in the myth, his understanding of his own humanity may have been altered. He may have learned much about the importance of justice to a good life and about the love of wisdom necessary for it. For the ruling image in the myth is neither the apportionment of *daimōnoi*, nor the apportionment of lots, nor of the granting of various rewards and the meting out of penalties—but it is wise choice of the best life available. Study and discipline are required in order choose well in Hades, just as they are on earth.

It may appear that the myth of Er combines the soul's immortality with the wages of justice. Tyrants like Ardiaeus suffer grievously in Hades (615c5–616b1), while noble souls who purify themselves of flaws like Odysseus do quite well. (620c3–d2) But immortality does not occur in the myth at all, which is concerned not with an afterlife (whether eternal or not) but with the ongoing education (*paideia*) of the soul in this life. Just as this life is finite, Hades is shot through and through with finitude: the image of the Fates in the Spindle of Necessity signals an irrevocable bond between choice and destiny; the choosing from an allotted number of lives indicates the specific possibilities and limits available both across lots and within each lot; the study of the behavior of individual souls testifies to the limited knowledge of the good life that each soul brings with it. Regarding the latter, Socrates says:

> From all this, he will be able to draw a conclusion and choose—in looking off, toward the nature of the soul—between the worse and the better life, calling worse the one that leads it toward becoming more unjust, and better to the one that leads to becoming juster. He will let everything else go. For we have seen that this is the most important choice for him in life and death. He must go to Hades adamantly holding to this *opinion* so he won't be daunted by wealth. . . (618d5–619a3; emphasis mine)

This choice of a just versus an unjust life is most important (*kratistē*) upon or under the earth, and it is presented as a choice that can always be made well or badly. Socrates calls this choice "the whole risk (*kindunos*) of a human being, friend Glaucon, as it seems." (618b6–7) The risk itself occurs as opinion, and in the myth has nothing to do with immortality.

Immortality comes up in the discussion only after the myth is finished, and is offered as a support for this soul-saving opinion and not at all as an enticement for believing it. If the myth persuades, then our souls will make a good crossing of the river Lethe, i.e. will find itself well-disposed toward the challenge of embodiment, which is the challenge of humanity. "But if we are persuaded by *me*," Socrates says, ". . .holding that the soul is immortal and capable of bearing all evils and all goods, we shall always keep to the upper road and practice justice with prudence. . ."(621c3–5; emphasis mine); and in so doing we'll be friends to ourselves and the gods (621c5–6), reap rewards and prizes (621d1), and do well above and below. (621d2–3)

While Socrates' "me" (*emoi*) distances his interpretation of the myth from the myth itself, his final words relate to it not as reasoned conclusion of immortality to mythical afterlife, but as bright tale of the fate of the soul to dark tale of that same fate. The core of the tale from either side is the same: the soul's finitude and ignorance in the face of its choices, and its need to seek what it lacks within itself from wherever it might find it. But as Socrates' activity both here and elsewhere makes clear, this serious pursuit is enacted playfully. This core is concealed in brightly presented but unfounded arguments for the soul's immortality and for its magnificent rewards if it is just, and in dark myths of the soul's destiny after death which promise somewhat more modest rewards better suited to life on earth. That the choice of the soul is located in a play of light and dark is entirely in keeping with Socrates' activity throughout the dialogues in which he appears.

The issue of immortality is clearly subordinate to the larger concern of a life lived justly, of a human being doing well. Insofar as we are persuaded of immortality, we are encouraged to act justly; and insofar as we are encouraged to act justly, we will do well. But Socrates is always concerned with doing well (*eu prattomen*), whether immortality is at issue or not: doing well animates all his activities, be they theoretical, ethical, political or aesthetic. So the issue of immortality is secondary, and makes no difference in the answering of questions concerning the best actions for human beings. In the blithe manner of its introduction into the *Republic*, in the loose argumentation offered in its behalf, in the myth of Er's treatment of the afterlife, and in the concluding parallel in which the journeys under and on the earth are presented as equivalent in their challenge, the immortality of the soul is at play in the dialogue—but not in a major way.

Immortality has less significance than the *eidē*[188] and than   Socratic ignorance in the *logoi* and *mythoi* of the dialogue. One cannot enter the dialogues without the *eidē*, however one decides their epistemological status and the nature and degree of their presence and absence. The questioning of the *eidē* and matters connected with them is indispensable to the disclosure of human knowledge and its limits, and is therefore indispensable to philosophy as practiced there. In the view here, they are not fixed points from which theories and doctrines are most properly derived but ruling images at play, opening up a field upon which human concerns can be treated appropriately. On this field one can speak properly and profitably about e.g. justice, beauty, goodness and seek them purposefully, although there is no full presence which would guarantee originary knowledge of them. Immortality is not essential to this field or to this task.

In the *Phaedrus*, immortality looks like it will be a major theme of Socrates' second speech on *Erōs*, with the lengthy proof basing the immortality of "all soul" (245c5) upon its eternal motion. But after one long paragraph, the issue of immortality drops loudly: "Concerning the immortality of the soul, this is enough." (246a3) Socrates then goes on to the more substantive matter of the *idea* of the soul, presenting it not as it is but "as it seems, which is something a human being could do. . ." (246a5–6)

In the *Phaedo*, Socrates prefaces his discussion of Simmias' and Cebes' concerns about death with a playful reference to Aristophanes, who "now. . .would not say that I am chattering and talking about things that do not concern me." (70c1–2) But ultimately, the arguments do not add up to much in terms of what is best for a human being to believe. After asserting misology as the greatest danger to the human soul and after urging his hearers not to distrust *logos* even in the face of a great many inadequate arguments, he says of his own attempts to argue for the soul's immortality:

> If what I say happens to be true, then it is admirable (*kalōs*) to be persuaded by
> it; and if there is nothing for me after death, at any rate I shall not be unpleasant

to my friends by my lamentations in these last moments. And this ignorance of mine will not last—that would be an evil—but would soon end. (91b2–9)

There is no worry over the outcome of the arguments, since nothing but good can come from Socrates' occupation in search of the best argument for immortality. Even a bad argument does no harm. Nothing but good, however, could come to him were he occupied with the search for the best argument on any subject: either he discovers a sound argument and it is admirable to be persuaded by him, or he falls short and can be brought before his ignorance. In the course of his search for such an argument on immortality, it becomes clear that its occasioning subject—death, specifically his own—seems to produce no more fear in Socrates than any other. He is either unafraid of death, or he does not impose his fear on others. But the issue for the interlocutors is precisely this fear, with the issues of immortality and the quality of arguments offered for it regarded as possible means of overcoming it.

In the *Apology*, Socrates speaks of a redirection of fear from fear of death to fear of doing injustice. Death's nature and consequences are unknown, and it is disgraceful to fear what one does not know. But it is known that to do injustice is disgraceful. Thus one should never fear death, but should only fear doing injustice. (28b3–9)[189] Fear itself is not disgraceful; it is one of the human things, part of the challenge of humanity. Socrates' call for its redirection is a playful and powerful one. The ease of assenting to his argument conceals the great difficulty of its acceptance in deed.

This ease and this difficulty meet in the *Phaedo*. In one of the dialogues' darker jests, the dying Socrates attempts to reassure his robust young companions that death is nothing to fear. After offering his second argument for the immortality of the soul, Socrates chides Simmias for the latter's childishness in supposing that the soul will disperse after death, and especially "in a high wind and not in calm weather." (77e1–2) Simmias concedes that there is "a child within which has such fears" (77e5) and entreats Socrates to help in persuading it "not to fear death as if it were a she-monster." ([*mormolukeia*]—77e6–7)

Socrates' answer: "You must *chant* (*epadein*) every day, until you charm the fear away." Then, after Simmias calls Socrates a "good singer" (*agathon epōdon*) (78a1) of such charms[190] and bemoans the incipient loss of his friend, Socrates counsels his interlocutors to search vigorously and everywhere for such an epode[191]: "There is nothing of greater necessity for which you could spend your money."(78a5–6) Thus, one who is capable of the chanting which is proper to the poetry of Homer[192] is the one who is most necessary of all. Socrates, whose services are had for free, is one such singer; part of the song of Socrates is that this song is most valuable of all.

In this light, the Socrates who practices music on the prompting of a dream is the one whose *logoi* are sufficient to charm away the fear of death. But the two arguments for the immortality of the soul, while good enough for Socrates who shows no such fear, are insufficient for Simmias and Cebes. This suggests, perhaps oddly, that somehow the physical bearing of Socrates—his self-presentation in *aisthēsis*—quiets the fear of death in his friends to some degree. As long as Socrates can be perceived by the senses, as long as singer and song can be seen and heard in their customary playful tranquillity, the fears of his friends are calmed.

Why is the service of chanting away fear so valuable that it requires one to spare no effort and no expense to secure it? (78a1–6) As we have seen, it is mistaken and disgraceful to fear death, as this fear announces that one claims to know what one does not know.[193] Chanting away fear chants away a large measure of error and disgrace. Further, the fear of death is a pretext for doing injustices of all kinds. The cause of this fear is the visible deterioration of the flesh, the visible extinction of the customary signs of life. This visible deterioration and extinction, for Simmias and Cebes as for most of their colleagues in the city, gives rise to the fear of utter annihilation which overcomes the force of Socrates' argument. This fear gives rise to the urgent need for an epode to quiet it, whoever that might be.

Concerning the quality of the arguments, it is enough to say that they are plausible even if they are not convincing. They are valid in structure but require a certain belief in the truth of key premises in each argument or significant part thereof. In order to regard at least one of the arguments as sound, one must believe that the dialogue establishes either that purification of and by thought occurs (65e6–66a10), or that opposites are generated from opposites (71a9–10), or that the *eidē* are recollected. (75c7–76a7) One or more of them might persuade someone predisposed to trust in *logos*, especially the third: the existence of the *eidē* is in some sense, if not entirely evident, at least strong and suggestive. But the arguments based upon such a premise will not convince anyone who is much afraid of death, who regards it as a child regards Mormon.[194] The argument premised upon evidence of bodily death in *aisthēsis* which concludes that the life of the soul is utterly terminated with this bodily death, while no more logically convincing (and perhaps less so) than the arguments for immortality in *logos*, preys upon the customary fear of death and its consequent distrust in *logos*.

So the genuine problem is not the logic of the arguments but trust (*pistis*) in the best *logos*. Its resolution also does not lie in logic, but in regarding death playfully. The Socrates who practices music meets death cheerfully, without any fear. Death to Socrates is like Mormon, a nonexistent monster who has been charmed and chanted away. But this chanting and charming must be seen as an encounter with *aisthēsis* by means of *aisthēsis*. The music of Socrates and his high-priced replacement-to-be must meet the fear of death in *aisthēsis*, where it resides most stubbornly and where arguments by themselves cannot reach.

At 70a1 Cebes says that humans are distrustful (*apistian*) in regard to the soul, fearing that it will be scattered and evaporated into nothing after death. This implies they are more trusting of matters given through *aisthēsis*. Socrates later says that this trust of the pleasures and pains of the body causes the soul to suffer "the greatest and most extreme evil" (83c2–3), namely the belief that the object which causes these pleasures and pains "is most distinct of all and most true of all." (83c7–8) This belief cements that same bondage to the body which works against trust in *logos*. (83d4ff)

The most remarkable feature of the bondage is that in significant measure, it is freely chosen:

. . .and philosophy sees (*katidousa*) that the most dreadful (*deinotēta*) thing about the imprisonment is that it occurs through desire (*epithumias*), so that the prisoner himself is the chief assistant (*sullēptōr*) in his own imprisonment. (82e5–83a2)

"Desire" refers to the part of the soul determined by the wants and needs of the body. The soul can be ruled by these desires, or can rule them (cf. Book IV of the *Republic*; the two "most vivid" desires are said at 437d2–5 to be hunger and thirst). They cannot rule without the cooperation of the rest of the soul, i.e. without the cooperation calculation and of spirit. How does the soul desire imprisonment? By the choice of putting calculation and spirit in the service of desire, the soul confers the aforementioned trust in *aisthēsis* as the orienting source of its life.

In the deed of conferring trust, the human being chooses the position as chief assistant to *aisthēsis*, helping the person's would-be captor achieve the status of actual captor. While there is no complete liberation from *aisthēsis* and desire, the prisoner did not and does not have to be a prisoner: he/she can withhold cooperation with desire, and so receive a measure of freedom from it, a reprieve from complete ensnarement in *aisthēsis*. The soul is free to trust either *logos* or desire, and the consequences of the decision as to where to place trust determines the quality of one's comportment toward death. This quality may be fearful, in the case of Simmias and Cebes; it may be cheerful in the case of Socrates; or it may fluctuate as one's trust fluctuates.

But how does one come to redirect one's trust from the evidence of *aisthēsis* to the evidence of *logos*? By which part of the soul can one stand outside the battle and choose to trust fairly good but not entirely convincing arguments over the stark but inarticulate evidence of *aisthēsis*? Pulled to *logos* on one side and desire on the other, isn't the human soul always on this battlefield by nature? The freeing from the battle for Socrates in the *Phaedo* occurs in terms of *music*: the "serious" music of philosophy, the "playful" music of popular taste, and the music Socrates playfully urges Simmias and Cebes to find. His insight into musical liberation comes neither from a rational pursuit nor from a direct bodily desire, but from a dream. Socrates' playful interpretation of his dream provides access to the transition from trust in *aisthēsis* to trust in *logos*, thus transforming the battlefield into a playground.

"Make music and work at it" (*mousikēn poiei kai ergazou*) (60e6–7), a voice in dream that came to him many times during his life, called for two kinds of activity according to Socrates: (1) practice philosophy, as you have been doing, and (2) make popular (*demōde*) music. He regarded the former as referring to the practice of philosophy his whole life, but obeys the latter call near the end of his life just to be safe. He never says, nor does he suggest that he disbelieves the former interpretation. He also never says, nor does he suggest, that the two interpretations contradict one another. (1) surely means that Socrates interpreted philosophical activity as musical, as given over to the Muses. It follows then, that the activities associated with philosophical *logos* in the dialogue, including the *elenchoi* and the arguments as well as the myths and the jests, are all given over to music in some way. (2) in Socrates' response does not mean just any popular music. His writing of a hymn to Apollo and his setting of Aesop's tales (*logous*) suggests a binding over of popular music to measure. Apollo playfully projects a divine image and Aesop's tales a human one of mindfulness toward what is proper for a human being.

This is why Socrates tells Simmias and Cebes to spare no expense in locating a musician who can charm away the fear of death: *logoi* separated from music and its playfulness, and charming music separated from measure, expose the soul to a fear that deforms it and to which it submits by placing its trust in the evidence of *aisthēsis*. As the interaction between Socrates, Simmias and Cebes has shown, mere rational argument is insufficient to break this Mormon-like fear of what one does not know. To say the same thing another way, the child within has to be quieted and encouraged, since it can neither be persuaded by argument or forced to give up its fear.

The bond of *aisthēsis* must be loosened through a certain kind of aesthetic play, presented here in the image of the musical Socrates. Given over to the Muse of philosophy and the popular music of measure he is said to have written, Socrates himself occurs as an artistic image within the philosophical and popular music of Plato's *Phaedo*. Insofar as this image occurs in *aisthēsis* and provides access through his music to a trust in *logos* and with it to the strength of the human soul, Socrates' cheerful tranquillity and playfulness image the music of which he speaks. The need for the continuation of this music-making has been projected into the future, after his death, as requiring some new wondrous and valuable epode. But Socrates inserts another suggestion: "And you must seek among yourselves, too: for it would not be easy to find people more able to do this than yourselves." (78a7–9)

From the untrusting (*apistian*) Simmias and Cebes to the wailing Apollodorus, the group assembled in Socrates' cell does not present a particularly promising group of candidates. But practice in the music of philosophical dialogue among themselves, which always seeks the best argument and the most just life, would release them from the fear of death they chose through the disorienting bond to *aisthēsis*. The dialogue provided by Phaedo provides images of at least much that is needed: the question "what does it mean? (*ti legei* ?)," which is asked of the dream and of every thought-provoking phenomenon; the question "what is it?" (*ti estin?*); the search for truth by means of the healthiest (*errōmenestaton*) *logos* and the trust in it; the *eidē* as hypothesized by this *logos*; the arguments and myths; and finally the playfulness and good cheer even, and perhaps especially, in the face of death. These elements, at once in the realm of sense but given over to philosophical *logos*, are repeatable without the actual physical presence of Socrates or the presence of Plato. Phaedo and Echecrates, the only genuine characters in the dialogue, show this by reenacting it for themselves.

In no case do we find epistemological certainty. But this is precisely why trust in *logos* is necessary, and why playfulness (and not the seriousness of certainty) given over to music and enacted in thoughtful *logos* becomes the principal mark of the philosopher in the Platonic dialogues.

CONCLUSION

A good deal of this work addresses itself to the poetic and musical side of the dialogues. The side concerned with arguments has been located within and alongside these non-rational elements, exhibiting their interplay. The ongoing mutual measuring by the two sides (and the related self-measuring within each side) is the thread which has held the various chapters together, just as it holds the Platonic dialogues together. There is no measuring of the measuring, nothing outside of the elements measuring and measured within the dialogues. I have called this internal self-reflective measuring movement the play of the Platonic dialogues.

Though I intend no irony when I say this, a rigorous reading of the Platonic text can come to no other conclusion than that this philosophical playfulness is its most distinctive, most basic, and most consistently discernible constituent. Through illustration and interpretation which is responsive to that play, and through argument, the pathway cleared by this work is offered both as an approach to the Platonic dialogues and to the way of philosophizing they present and enact.

Toward the end of the Foreword, four standard saws about the dialogues were listed:

1) The dialogues attempt to replace mythical explanations with rational

ones.

2) The *eidē* are ideal objects of some kind.

3) Virtue is knowledge.

4) The dialogues advocate some form of censorship.

All four of these are large issues which have commanded much attention from learned and worthy minds, so it may seem cavalier to dismiss them all in a few short paragraphs. But the results of *The Play of the Platonic Dialogues*, based upon clear textual evidence, make the following brief survey possible.

1) The dialogues abound with mythical material which is crucial to them. The *Republic*, which many regard as the most important one, concludes with a great myth; the *Timaeus* is almost entirely myth; others quite clearly revolve around mythical material. (See esp. Chapters 2 ,4 , 6–10)

2) The *eidē* are not "objects" at all, and to call them *ideal* is mere redundancy. They are beheld in their absence. They are what we suppose we would see if we had *nous*. If we are forced to speak of them out of their context in the dialogues, we might call them myths of reason. (see esp. Chapters 3, 4, 12)

3) Virtue is *not* knowledge, but a certain posture toward ignorance. (See esp. Chapters 2, 4)

4) The advocacy of censorship is primarily play. Its context of a myth told within a myth for the sake of an unjust city, and the fact that the same charges levelled against poetry are levelled against Socrates (and still others), guarantees its non-seriousness. (See esp. Chapters 5–8, 11)

While these "issues" can be and are surely detached, isolated and treated on their own terms in that way, it is a large blunder to ascribe this way of philosophizing to the Platonic dialogues. There is no doubt that their treatment of many issues, and many of their arguments, bequeathed much to the discipline of philosophy. But separating them from the playfulness in which they are situated has separated much contemporary philosophy from its greatest gift.

Recalling Sallis' words cited in the Foreword, "the interpreter [of Plato] must become—though in a different way—one of the interlocutors of the dialogue." (p. 22) The challenge: to be drawn, like the latecoming Socrates and the still later arriving Alcibiades, into the play of the *logoi*.

WORKS CITED

Burnet, John, *Platonis Opera*, 5 vols. (Oxford: Clarendon Press, 1900-07).

Translations

The Collected Dialogues of Plato, ed. Hamilton & Cairns (Princeton: Princeton University Press, 1989).

Meno, tr. Grube (Indianapolis: Hackett Publishing Co., 1984).

Plato, vol. I, tr. Fowler (Cambridge: Harvard University Press, The Loeb Classical Library, 1914).

Plato, vol. VII, tr. R. G. Bury (Cambridge: Harvard University Press, 1952).

The Republic of Plato, Bloom, Allan, tr., (New York: Basic Books, 1968).

The Symposium and the Phaedrus: Plato's Erotic Dialogues, tr. W.S. Cobb (Albany: SUNY Press, 1993).

Interpretive Works

Arieti, James A., *Interpreting Plato: The Dialogues as Drama* (Savage: Rowman & Littlefield, 1991).

Aristophanes, *Clouds*, ed. Dover (Oxford: Oxford at the Clarendon Press, 1968).

Bloom, Allan, *The Republic of Plato, translated with notes and an interpretive essay* (New York & London: Basic Books, 1968).

Boudouris, K., ed., *The Philosophy of Socrates: Elenchus, Ethics and Truth* (Athens: Kardamista Press, 1992).

Burger R, *The Phaedo: A Platonic Labyrinth* (New Haven: Yale University Press, 1984).

Derrida, Jacques, *Dissemination*, tr. Johnson, B. (Chicago: University of Chicago Press, 1981).

_____*La Dissemination* (Paris: Editions du Seuil, 1972).

_____"Structure, Sign and Play in the Discourse of the Human Sciences," in Donato and Macksey, ed., *The Structuralist Controversy* (Baltimore: Johns Hopkins University Press, 1972).

Diels, Hermann, *Die Fragmente der Vorsokratiker*, Band I (Berlin-Grunewald: Weidmannsche Verlagsbuchhandlung, 1951).

Elias, Julius, *Plato's Defence of Poetry* (Albany: SUNY Press, 1984).

Friedländer, Paul, *Plato*, vol. 2, tr. Hans Meyerhoff, New York: (Bollingen Series LIX, Pantheon Books, 1938).

Gadamer, H. G., *Dialogue and Dialectic*, tr. P.C. Smith (New Haven: Yale University Press, 1980).

Griswold, C. L., *Self-Knowledge in Plato's Phaedrus* (New Haven: Yale University Press, 1986).

Hegel, G.W.F., *Lectures on the History of Philosophy*, vol. 1., tr. Haldane (New York: The Humanities Press, 1963).

_____*Phänomenologie des Geistes* (Hamburg: Felix Meiner Verlag, 1952).

Heidegger, Martin, "Platons Lehre von der Wahrheit," in *Wegmarken* (Frankfurt am Main: Vittorio Klostermann, 1967).

Irwin, Terence, *Plato's Moral Theory: The Early and Middle Dialogues* (Oxford: Oxford University Press, 1977).

Klein, Jakob, *A Commentary upon Plato's Meno* (Chapel Hill: The University of North Carolina Press, 1965).

Levinson, Ronald B, *In Defense of Plato* (New York: Russell & Russell, 1970).

Liddell & Scott, *A Greek-English Lexicon*, 7th edition (Oxford: Clarendon Press, 1961, original edition, 1843).

Mattei, Jean Francois, "The Theatre of Myth in Plato," in Griswold, C. L., ed., *Platonic Writings: Platonic Readings* (New York: Routledge, 1988).

Miller, M. H., *Plato's Parmenides* (Princeton: Princeton University Press, 1986).

Murray, Gilbert, *Aristophanes* (New York: Russell & Russell, Inc., 1964).

Nietzsche, Friedrich, *The Birth of Tragedy*, tr. Kaufmann (New York: Vintage Books, 1967).

Popper, Karl, *The Open Society and its Enemies* (Princeton: Princeton University Press, 1950).

Quine, W. V. O., *Theories and Things* (Cambridge: Belknap Harvard, 1981).

Rorty, Richard, *Philosophy and the Mirror of Nature* (Princeton: Princeton University Press, 1979.)

Rosen, Stanley, *Plato's Symposium* Second Edition (New Haven: Yale University Press, 1987).

_____*Plato's Sophist* (New Haven & London: Yale University Press, 1983).

_____*The Quarrel between Philosophy and Poetry* (New York: Routledge, 1988).

Sallis, John, *Being and Logos: The Way of Platonic Dialogue* (Atlantic Highlands: Humanities Press International, Inc., 1986.) (Original edition Pittsburgh: Duquesne University Press, 1975).

_____*The Gathering of Reason* (Athens: Ohio University Press, 1980).

Shorey, Paul, *The Unity of Plato's Thought* (Chicago: Archon Books, 1988).

Strauss, Leo, *Studies in Platonic Political Philosophy* (Chicago: U. of Chicago Press, 1986).

Taylor, A. E., *Plato: The Man and his Work* (London: Methuen & Co. Ltd., 1952).

_____*Socrates*, (New York: D. Appleton and Co., 1933).

Vlastos, Gregory, "The Paradox of Socrates," in Vlastos, *The Philosophy of Socrates* (Notre Dame: U. of Notre Dame Press, 1980).

Whitehead, Alfred North, *Adventures of Ideas* (New York: The MacMillan Company, 1961).

Wild, John, "Plato as an Enemy of Democracy: A Rejoinder," in Thorson, T. L., ed., *Plato: Totalitarian or Democrat* (Englewood Cliffs: Prentice Hall, 1963).

ENDNOTES

Foreword

1. *Paizō* means to play in the most general sense; *pais* (either gender) means child; *paidia* means game or pastime or sport; *paideia* means rearing or education (the verb is *paideuō*).

2. Among the classical commentators on Plato, Paul Friedländer gives play the most prominence. In his three volume *Plato* (tr. Hans Meyerhoff, New York: Bollingen Series LIX, Pantheon Books, 1938) play is united with seriousness throughout. At one point, he observes that "play and seriousness are twins" (I, p. 93). Ultimately, play is informed by and in service to seriousness for Friedländer (I, p. 124–5).

    This belief, together with his view of poetry as aimed primarily at pleasure and philosophy at seriousness, cannot be adopted here. But his recognition of the prominence of play in Plato, and especially his joining it so intimately with seriousness, makes him a valuable precursor and places this work in his debt.

3. Sallis, John, *Being and Logos: The Way of Platonic Dialogue*, (Atlantic Highlands: Humanities Press International, Inc., 1986). (Original edition Pittsburgh: Duquesne University Press, 1975).

    As this book goes to press, a new edition of this work has appeared; the pagination of the main text is exactly the same as the second edition: *Being and Logos: Reading the Platonic Dialogues*, third edition (Bloomington and Indianapolis: Indiana University Press, 1996).

4. See *Theaetetus*, 155d2–5.

5. Sallis, op. cit., p. 16.

6. *Ibid.*, p. 15.

7. Of course, the interpretation/translation of this little Greek word is a great matter, and the decision made with regard to it may well shape the interpretation as a whole very decisively. Its original kinship with *mythos* is in very little doubt, but the proper relation of *mythos* to *logos*, especially in the Platonic dialogues, is a difficult matter, and surely impossible to determine apart from its enactment in the dialogues themselves. This issue surfaces strongly in Chapter 2, and receives thematic treatment in Part II of this book (especially Chapters 5 and 6).

    While I am quite sympathetic to the efforts of Heidegger to think *logos* back to its originary sense as "gathering," a sense renewed by Sallis in the title of his own *The Gathering of Reason* (Athens: Ohio University Press, 1980), I will not read it into my own interpretation in advance. *Logos* will occur in *The Play of the Platonic Dialogues* with as few predeterminations of any kind as possible; that is, it will be allowed to occur at play in the dialogues, and whatever shows itself out of that play will be duly noted.

8. Sallis, op. cit., p. 21–22.

9. Sallis' triad consists of *logos*, *mythos* and *ergon* (deed). Deeds (*erga*) include events which occur in the dialogues which are provoked by *mythoi* and *logoi*, such as dramatic unveilings and such as characters behaving differently toward one another in light of what is said in the conversation. *Ergon* also refers to the ultimate deed of recollection in the soul. (*Being and Logos*, p. 12–21) Play is "the final feature. . .to which we need to attend" (21) in his introduction. I have allowed the dimension of deeds (*erga*) to be absorbed into the play of the dialogues.

10. "The Socratic Concept of Truth", found in *The Philosophy of Socrates: Elenchus, Ethics and Truth*, ed. K. Boudouris (Athens: Kardamista Press, 1992), p. 58.

11. *Ibid.*, p. 56.

12. Sallis, op. cit., p. 22.

Chapter One

13. Whitehead, Alfred North, *Adventures of Ideas* (New York: The MacMillan Company, 1961), p. 203.

14. *Ibid.*, p. 203.

15. Derrida, Jacques, "Structure, Sign and Play in the Discourse of the Human Sciences," in *The Structuralist Controversy*, ed. Donato & Macksey (Baltimore: Johns Hopkins University Press, 1972), p. 264–5.

16. Rorty, Richard, *Philosophy and the Mirror of Nature* (Princeton: Princeton University Press, 1979), p. 392.

17. *Ibid.*, p. 391.

18. Quine, W. V., *Theories and Things* (Cambridge: Belknap Harvard, 1981), p. 192.

19. *Ibid.*, p. 192.

20. Sallis, *Being and Logos*, p. 51.

21. *Ibid.*, p. 22n.

22. In the *Gorgias*, Socrates upbraids the eristic Callicles in a way which might seem that play is an inappropriate response to a serious subject: "By Friendship, you must not play with me. . ." (500b5–7) and "don't take what I propose as playing. . ."(500b7–c1), urging him not to give answer contrary to his opinion. However, Callicles' play is inappropriate not because it is play, but because it is intentionally false, i.e. unbound to truth.

    It should be noted that while Socrates insists upon the high seriousness of his and Callicles' discussion of the kind of life one should live, the *Gorgias* concludes with his telling of a playful myth which plays, among other things, on poetical images drawn from Homer. (See chapter 7 for an exploration of the Homer/Plato relation in terms of play, and Chapter 11 for a treatment of imitation and play in a more general way.)

23. Both this passage (and its general relation to *Ecclesiazousai*) receive further comment in Chapter 8, p. 118ff.

24. The great contribution to philosophy of this unfairly neglected dialogue is discussed in Chapter 7.

25. J.A. Arieti is a recent writer who, in his book on individual dialogues entitled *Interpreting Plato: The Dialogues as Drama* (Savage: Rowman & Littlefield, 1991) properly noted the importance of play: ". . .Plato means what he says when he claims that his dialogues are play. . ."

    One dialogue he omits, however, is the *Laws*. So it is not surprising that he continues the above thought with: ". . .and I shall look for the serious point that emerges in the play." (p. 8)

26. See Foreword, p. 6, where the treatment by Socrates of death as a plaything is introduced.

27. For a treatment of the forms in terms of play, see Chapter 3; this central matter will be addressed frequently thereafter.

Chapter Two

28. Sallis, *Being and Logos*, p. 16. He goes on to say that this contrast should not be too rigidly drawn, and to suggest that it is a contrast *within* what is said.

29. Plato, *Symposium* 203b1–204a7.

30. "Back then, since they weren't wise the way you young people are today, people were content in their simplicity to listen to an oak tree or a rock, if it spoke the truth." (*Phaedrus* 275b7–c1)

31. See Chapter 12, p. 181ff., for the treatment of trust in the *Phaedo*, which thematizes trust in *logoi* generally.

32. The sun, divided line and cave images, from 506d6 in Book VI through 518d7 in Book VII. This same section will be treated in the next chapter, where the corresponding brightness is also established.

33. See also Chapter 3, p. 44–49, where the relation of the line and the image of the cave is treated in terms of the general image-play of the dialogues.

34. See page 47 for a full citation.

35. The progress of the *Republic* from the gates of Hades in Piraeus to the myth of Er through several stops under the earth might be seen as a vivid image of the recurring provocation of the dark, as is Socrates' remark in the *Phaedo* that philosophy—an activity bound to the recognition of ignorance—is practice for dying.

36. Both the various qualifiers and the self-undermining character of the divided line are treated extensively in Chapter 3.

37. Irwin, Terence, *Plato's Moral Theory: The Early and Middle Dialogues* (Oxford: Oxford University Press, 1977), p. 221.

38. *Ibid.*, p. 223. The account leading to this citation runs from p. 221–223.

39. *Ibid.*, p. 223.

40. Jakob Klein astutely notes the importance of this freely given protestation of ignorance, its contribution to the learning process, and its favorable reflection upon the soul of the slave boy: "To submit oneself to refutation without getting angry and feeling disgraced is the first and indispensable step. . ." For the learning process to go forward, "A great deal, then, must depend not only upon the quality of the teacher but also on the quality of the learner." [*A Commentary upon Plato's Meno* (Chapel Hill:The University of North Carolina Press, 1965), p. 105–6.]

41. All three passages in this paragraph are found in Rosen, Stanley, *The Quarrel Between Philosophy and Poetry* (New York: Routledge, 1988), p. 26.

42. For example, *Phaedrus*, 269d6–8: To attain the art [of rhetoric], the way to reach it does not appear, in my opinion, to be the *methodos* of Lysias or Thrasymachos. (Interestingly, Socrates recommends leisurely talk and stargazing to Phaedrus.); *Republic* 510c5: ". . .the geometers treat. . .the figures, the three forms of angles, and others akin to these according to the *methodos* of each." *Statesman*, 286d4–5: "First we must honor the *methodos* capable of distinguishing according to form." In each example, there is an echo of the root *hodos* which means "pathway" or "road," suggesting a somewhat looser (but no less rigorous) sense than that of a procedure fixed in advance by rules.

43. Irwin, op. cit., p. 170–1.

44. Irwin, op. cit., p. 168

45. Rosen, Stanley, *Plato's Symposium*, Second Edition (New Haven: Yale University Press, New Haven, 1987), p. 338.

46. *Ibid.*, p. 282.

47. See Chapter 4, p. 60–61.

48. This distinction, first given major impetus by Gregory Vlastos, animates a good deal of Anglo-American Plato scholarship. Although much work is undertaken in serene confidence concerning both the reality and the philosophical importance of this distinction, there is little if any textual basis in the dialogues for asserting it. Plato remarks in the *Second Letter* that ". . .there is not and will not be any written work of Plato's own. What are now called his are the work of a Socrates become beautiful and new." (314c2–4) In light of this passage, whether interpreted straightforwardly or reflected back upon itself, the ascription of definite views to definite personages is perilous at least, if not out of the question altogether.

    And quite apart from the question of the authenticity of the Letters, Plato never speaks in any of the dialogues and no views are ever ascribed to him. (See Sallis, *Being and Logos*, p. 2–3)

49. Rosen's *Plato's Sophist* (New Haven and London: Yale University Press, 1983), especially his argument that Plato is not addressing logical predication in this dialogue, is a major contribution.

50. Cf. *Meno* 79d7–80b7.

51. See Chapter 4, p. 60-63.

52. Its immediate surroundings are the preceding encounter with Agathon and the subsequent entrance of Alcibiades; the speech cannot be detached from these and regarded as a doctrine without making nonsense of these surroundings.

    More generally, the speech was told to Apollodorus, who is known as a madman, by Aristodemus. The latter accompanied Socrates to the symposium but fell asleep from drunkenness somewhere in the midst of the speeches. This measures the Diotima-inspired speech of Socrates as well as the others, giving the *Symposium* its own peculiar kind of reliability. This issue recurs in another context also at pp. 60–63.

53. By this I mean that the condition of embodiment is leapt over as if it were no obstacle at all, in the manner of Socrates swinging from the air and looking down with disdain on mere mortals in Aristophanes' *Clouds*. Chapter 8 will treat the relation of philosophy and comedy in Plato.

54. John Sallis has suggested that to the head correspond arguments, to the feet myths, to the body as a whole the deeds, and to the extremities the various jests, byplay, etc. See Sallis, John, *Being and Logos*, p. 14–19.

55. See especially Chapter 6, where the intertwining of *mythos* and *logos* is shown in "large letters" in the city.

56. See especially Chapter 9, where the dialogical recoil of the written word upon itself is shown to image the movement of the philosophical soul in the deed of recollection.

Chapter Three

57. See also Chapter 2, p. 27.

58. "Those who are able to approach the fair itself and see it by itself [are] rare. . ."
     (476b10–11)

59. In Chapter 8, this passage recurs, playing a role in the unfolding of comedy. This
     chapter prepares the way.

60. See Sallis, *Being and Logos*, p. 401–455.

61. Sallis, *Being and Logos*, p. 448f.

62. In the *Philebus*, Socrates treats *nous* with a similar mixture of casualness and
     earnestness:

     > For all the wise agree, glorifying themselves in earnest, that in *nous* we
     > have the king of heaven and earth. And probably (*isōs*) (!) they are right.
     > But I should like us, if you don't mind, to make a fuller investigation of the
     > kind in question itself. (28c6–9)

     And the "fuller investigation" lands *nous* in third place among desirable
     possessions for a human being, surpassing pleasure but "trailing" the (difficult to
     name) *to metrion* (the measured) and *to kairion* (the appropriate) deemed worthiest,
     and *to teleon* (the fulfilled) and to hikanon (the sufficient)—third, as Socrates divines
     (*manteia*)(!), is *nous* and *phronēsis*. (66a4–b6)

63. See Chapter 12 on "Play and Immortality" for a fuller discussion of this issue.

Chapter Four

64. Socrates gives a funeral oration, but there is no funeral. The speech which honors
     the specific dead of Athens is, in fact, a portable one: from Pericles, to Aspasia, to
     Socrates—but Socrates often forgot it when it was taught to him. (cf. 235e1 and ff.)

65. Laches and Nicias are worthy generals and brave men, but they are unable to say
     what courage is; the supposed unity of *logos* (word) and *ergon* (deed), is disrupted.
     It will happen again, along somewhat different but related lines, in the discussion of
     the excellent rhapsode in the *Ion* who does not know the meaning of what he recites.
     See Chapter 6.

66. Virtue is not defined in any other dialogue, either.

67. Paul Shorey cites the *Meno* in support of this venerated thesis, but the two passages
     he selects contradict it. The first, "97B," shows neither that "persistent right opinion
     presupposes knowledge in its teachers" nor that "the highest rule of conduct must be
     deduced from and referred to a rational apprehension of ultimate good." Instead, it
     shows that someone without knowledge (of the road to Larissa) but with true opinion
     can be just as good a guide to action as the one who knows.

"100A: *hoios kai allon poiesai*, etc." is likened to mythical Tiresias. Even within the myth, his "knowledge" was nothing like a rational apprehension of ultimate good. [(*The Unity of Plato's Thought* (Chicago: Archon Books, 1988, p. 10.)]

68. This "interlude" could well be interpreted as Socrates' true speech, and is best seen as belonging together with the more celebrated Diotima-speech. *Elenchos* and *mythos* could then be seen as at play.

69. Death in Phaedrus' speech, weak *logos* in Pausanias', discord in Eryximachus', primordial woundedness in Aristophanes', lightness (although there really is no negativity) in Agathon's and mortality in Socrates'.

70. It can also be interpreted as a restoration of measure which is entirely disruptive.

71. As M. H. Miller points out, there are (also) clear references to Parmenides' "Proem," and to aspects of the *Republic*. See *Plato's Parmenides* (Princeton: Princeton University Press, 1986), p. 15–25.

72. This issue was first introduced in Chapter 2, p. 25 and will be treated throughout the book, but most thoroughly in the final chapter, p. 181ff.

73. The same can be said of friendship (*philia*) in the *Lysis*. Just as with virtue in the *Meno*, the outcome does not bring the speakers any closer to an account of friendship. Its last line reads: "We have not yet been able to learn what a friend is (*hosti estin to philos*)."

    Yet friendship is enacted by Socrates toward Lysis and Menexenus, in such a way as to provoke the ongoing thoughtful growth of the two youths in the absence of an account at that time.

74. See Chapter 2, p. 50ff., for a discussion of healthy *logos* and the *eidē*.

Chapter Five

75. In the case of poetics/ethics/psychology, the distance between the dialogues and our contemporary concerns is more obvious, although no less striking.

76. "Apology" is understood here in the Greek sense as a speaking forth, an explanation, a "defense."

77. Allan Bloom, in his notes to his Plato translation (Book V, note 36, p. 460), points out correctly that the coincidence, or "falling together," of philosophy and political power indicates that there is "no necessary connection" between them. He uses the looseness of their connection to distinguish Plato from what he calls the Enlightenment view, according to which an improvement in knowledge transforms political society for the better. The note concludes by denying, in this light, that Plato is an optimist.

    This conclusion, however, does not nearly go far enough. There is rather a necessary *disconnect* between philosophical natures and natures which acquire political power. In disjoining the two realms, this disconnect places the matter beyond both optimism and pessimism.

78. See Sallis, *Being and Logos*, p. 369-71 on desire, the city, and philosophy.

79. See also Chapter 8, p. 119f. for a discussion of sacred marriage in the context of comedy.

80. In this context of Book X, I will translate *logos* and its variants as "argument" and its variants, in order to set it off clearly from musical activity.

81. An apology in prose is an acceptable supplement. (607d6–8)

82. The philosophic nature hates the willing lie, the kind which the king must tell; the poet is not willing in that manipulative sense, but inspired.

83. This issue will be treated in a more thoroughgoing fashion at the beginning of Chapter 7, where the relation of poetry and philosophy is the express theme.

84. See Chapter 8, p. 114f., for further discussion of chanting, music and *logos*.

Chapter Six

85. For example, the most provocative account of Plato's "political philosophy" published in the last half of this century is Karl Popper's *The Open Society and its Enemies* (Princeton: Princeton University Press, 1950). In it, he argues that Plato's notion of justice is based upon class privilege and inequality, features contempt for the individual citizen as individual, is racist, and advocates a totalitarianism which would not be incompatible with Nazi Germany's. *In Defense of Plato*, by Ronald B. Levinson (New York: Russell & Russell, 1970), attempts a definitive and thorough answer to Popper's charge and the charges of others who embraced the Popperian view.

    In his way of viewing Plato, Levinson notes Popper's "perverse literal-mindedness in construing Plato's metaphors." (p. 441) Other commentators regard the *Republic* as an ideal with qualities to be emulated to the degree that they can and not as political program (see note 91 below).

    This much can be said for Popper's view: if the play of the dialogue is set aside entirely, along with all of the earlier material concerning the education of the guardians, concerning the relation of the image of the city to the individual soul especially at the close of Book IX but also throughout, concerning the matters raised in Book V which call into question the city's possibility—then Popper's view makes sense. But in light of this play, which permeates the dialogue and which is signalled within it at every turn, his charge simply falls apart.

86. Sallis, op. cit., p. 1.

87. See Chapter 2, p. 31, and endnote 48 for material on Platonic authorship.

88. See Chapter 12, p. 179ff., where the redirection of fear is seen as central to Socratic philosophical practice.

89. See Chapter 5, p. 71ff for the earlier treatment of this issue in the light of the crafting of this education in terms of a rejected definition of justice.

90. Cf. *Apology*, 22b10–c5; and esp. *Ion* 533c9–535a2.

91. For a full lexicographic treatment of the two key words, see *A Greek-English Lexicon*, compiled by Liddell & Scott, 7th edition (Oxford: Clarendon Press, 1961) (original edition 1843). The *logos* listing is found on p. 1057–9; the *mythos* listing is found on p. 1151.

92. *Metenegkontes*, from *metapherein* which means "to carry over," and which is the root of our "metaphor."

93. Here I am thinking of the textual phenomenon of the philosopher-king, although I do not believe this to be an actual possibility given what else is said in the text. See Chapter 5, p. 73–76.

94. See also Chapter 3, p. 48f., for a discussion of the city in *logos* fashioned apart from the *eidē*, and Chapter 5, p. 69f. for a discussion of the indeterminacy of the location of the Platonic city.

95. E.g. John Wild, "The *Republic* is a universal ideal to be approximated in the concrete realm of flux. . .It is no more a closed society than any other rationally articulated social ideal." [in *Plato: Totalitarian or Democrat*, ed. T. L. Thorson (Englewood Cliffs: Prentice Hall, 1963, p. 124)]; "The actualization of the best regime proves indeed to be impossible or at least extremely improbable; only a diluted version of that political order which strictly corresponds to natural right can in reason be expected." [Strauss, Leo, *Studies in Platonic Political Philosophy* (Chicago: U. of Chicago Press, 1986), p. 39.]; and Levinson, op. cit., p. 440, ". . .the *Republic* is a sketch of a fully ideal community, the limiting case as it were. . ."

    All three commentators are sympathetic to Plato, and in different ways relocate the dialogues into philosophy in its traditional sense as the pursuit of wisdom. At the very least, Popper's challenge provoked a response from some Plato scholars which recalled and refocussed the basic role and orientation to the dialogues. My difference with them on the nature of the ideal remains within this focus.

96. See Liddell & Scott, op. cit., p. 817; also *The Compact Oxford English Dictionary*, Second Edition (Complete Text Reproduced Micrographically) (Oxford: Clarendon Press, 1994), p. 819.

97. Though the dating of Homer's epics is a difficult task, it can be said with some confidence that the most recent plausible date is the 7th century or 8th century B.C., and that the Trojan war took place many centuries earlier—if it took place at all.

Chapter Seven

98. I take the phrase from Book X of the *Republic*, and understand Homer to be their "father," as it is said in the dialogue.

99. Two samples of the conventional wisdom: A.E. Taylor: "[Socrates] is seriously proposing to censure just what we consider to be the imperishable contributions of Athens to the art and literature of the world, because he holds that they have tendencies which are unfavourable to the development of the highest development

of moral personality." [*Plato: The Man and his Work* (London: Methuen & Co. Ltd., 1952), p. 279–80.] Even the astute Friedländer wrote ". . .there is no place for any mimetic art and its ancestor Homer. . .This, to begin with, must be taken quite seriously." (op. cit., v. 1, p. 121–2) Two harbingers of its demise: ". . .Plato's writings contain and imply an acknowledgement of the indispensability of poetry." Elias, Julius, *Plato's Defence of Poetry* (Albany: SUNY Press, 1984), p. 1; the book emphasizes the positive contribution of myths to the pursuit of truth and of a good society. Jean Francois Mattei also grants intrinsic centrality to myth in his "The Theatre of Myth in Plato," found in *Platonic Writings: Platonic Readings*, ed. Griswold, C. L. (New York: Routledge, 1988), p. 66–83.

100. See Chapter 2, p. 24, for a list of such incontrovertible Platonic beliefs and obligations.

101. This is why the issue of whether a city can take philosophy in hand and not be destroyed, which Socrates raises as 497d8–9, is taken so seriously. The two images at play are the philosopher-king, in which philosophy and political power are conjoined, and the philosopher as necessary underminer of the received opinions and practices of the city, in which they are disjoined.

102. See Chapter 5, p. 69f., where the ambiguous location of the Platonic city is discussed.

103. This is where Gadamer's interpretation of the *Republic* goes badly astray. Instead of noting the self-reflexivity of the Socratic "complaint," he reads it as the direct statement of the Platonic "position": "The poet. . .is said to be a sophist and a magician who produces only deceptive appearances of things. And what is worse, he ruins the soul by stirring up in it the whole range of its passions. Hence it proves necessary to exile all the 'sweet muses' from the state. . That *in nuce* is the Platonic position." [*Dialogue and Dialectic*, tr. P.C. Smith (New Haven: Yale University Press, 1980], p. 46.] This misstep requires a tortuous line of argument which leads to the suggestion that the dialogues themselves are "the true poetry" because they are "in jest and only meant to be in jest" (p. 71). But this is precisely the Socratic critcism of the poets.

104. Liddell & Scott, op. cit., p. 855.

105. See *Gorgias* 523a2–3, where Socrates invokes Homer's authority to prove that he is speaking "the real truth" (*hōs alēthē gar onta*) in his myth; and with somewhat less import at 524d7, where Homer is appealed to as an authority on Hades. (See also Chapter 11, p. 166ff.)

106. Three telling silences occur in the *Lesser Hippias*: (1) the silence in the face of the uninterrupted assault of Hippias' confident speech at the dialogue's outset; (2) the silence at the end in the face of the wandering, which is the fate of human beings and which precludes too much confidence; (3) the threatened silence of Hippias in the middle, which Socrates and his philosophical "embassy" interrupts.
      The silences occur (1) after what seems to have been a long rhetorical onslaught from Hippias, (2) after a long ironic and philosophical piece of rhetoric from Socrates and (3) after the discussion leads to a conclusion that neither can accept.

In all cases the soul seeks to step back and redirect itself. These telling silences which interrupt the flow of noise and/or confusion also belong to the play of philosophy and poetry as granting a space which makes this play possible.

107. *Plagchthe*, from *plazō*, the epic form of *planasthai*, belongs to the description of Odysseus which opens the *Odyssey* (Book I, line 2).

108. After praising Achilles in argument, Socrates wins a playful victory over proud Hippias—using the image of Odysseus originally championed by the latter. Socrates' thoughtful and playful relation to poetic matters shows itself here once again.

Chapter Eight

109. See Chapter 3, p. 43-44, where Socrates' greed for images is at play with the apparent demand for intelligibility free of images.

110. See *Apology* 28d1–5, where Socrates cites *Iliad*, Book 18, l. 96f; and 34d3–4, where he quotes *Odyssey*, Book 19, l. 163).

111. Aristophanes, *Clouds*, ed. Dover, Oxford at the Clarendon Press, (Oxford: 1968), l. 169–174.

112. *Ibid.*, l. 186–194.

113. *Ibid.*, l. 1088–1104.

114. See Chapter 7, p. 101ff.

115. One such issue concerns the meaning and intention of the Aristophanic parody, and the role of the historical circumstances surrounding the production of *Clouds* and the trial of Socrates some two decades later. Whether Aristophanes' intention was benign and the meaning playful or the reverse—and whether as Murray maintains, "the whole trouble and danger came from the change in atmosphere. In 423 these charges (i. e. the old accusations) were jokes. In 399 they were not jokes at all," [Murray, Gilbert, *Aristophanes* (New York: Russell & Russell, Inc., 1964), p. 99.] or whether some less innocent explanation accounts for Aristophanes' status as an old accuser, the *Apology* shows Socrates fighting with this image as he fights for his life. But how can one fight with an image?

It is not unusual to view this battle as having Aristophanes on one side and Plato and Xenophon on the other, with the reputation of Socrates at stake and with one or the other having more justice on its side; there are also variants within this scenario, such as *Clouds* being a friendly but misunderstood satire or Socrates having changed from a sophist to a sage in the intervening 24 years. (Cf. Dover, K., "Socrates in the Clouds," found in Vlastos, op. cit., p. 67f.)

116. See also Chapter 3, p. 30ff., where Stanley Rosen's thoughtful treatment of the quarrel is discussed.

117. . . .and which conviction is "avenged" not long after by the prosecution and death of Meletus and Anytus.

118. See Chapter 5, p. 78ff.

119. Vlastos, Gregory, "The Paradox of Socrates," found in Vlastos, G., *The Philosophy of Socrates* (Notre Dame: U. of Notre Dame Press, 1980), p. 4.

120. *Ibid.*, p. 17–20.

121. *Ibid.*, p. 18.

122. Aristophanes, op. cit., l. 1014.

123. See p. 84ff. for the earlier discussion of Mormon, the she-monster.

124. See Chapter 12 for an extensive treatment of philosophy, play and death.

125. e.g. Sallis, op. cit., p. 377n and Bloom. op. cit. (in his "Interpretive Essay"), p. 380–1.

126. See Chapter 5, p. 74f. for the discussion of the impossibility of the two natures "falling together."

127. "So, when in someone [the desires] have flowed toward learning and all that's like it, I suppose that they would. . .forsake all those pleasures which come through the body—if he isn't a counterfeit but a true philosopher."
    "Most necessary." (485d10–e2)
    But Socrates has disqualified himself from the ranks of such true philosophers. He came to Piraeus that evening to watch religious processions and to see a torch race on horseback, and on other occasions has clearly enjoyed eating, drinking and associating with the beautiful.

128. Aristophanes, op. cit. l. 225.

Chapter Nine

129. See Chapter 2, p. 26, and especially p. 37f., for the original discussion.

130. See Chapter 2, p. 26f. and p. 37f. for the earlier discussion of strangeness.

131. See Griswold, C. L., *Self-knowledge in Plato's Phaedrus*, Yale University Press (New Haven: 1986), p. 39–43 for a thoughtful discussion of Typhon.

132. The Boreas and Oreithuia myth is a tale of love's transport, the theme of Socrates' second speech.

133. An earlier sample was provided in Chapter 1, p. 12-13; a brief discussion follows this sample.

134. Tr. Johnson, B., University of Chicago Press (Chicago: 1981). Original: Derrida, Jacques, *La Dissemination*, Editions du Seuil (Paris: 1972).

135. *Ibid.*, p. 111.

136. Derrida's view of written speech as prior to spoken need not be engaged here, where the issue is the Platonic text itself and what is said in it. It is clear, however, that whatever the merits of this influential view, it is an external imposition upon these texts on its face.

137. *Ibid.*, p.103.

138. Cf. p. 81–82.

139. Sallis, op. cit., p. 1.

140. Heidegger, Martin, "Platons Lehre von der Wahrheit," in *Wegmarken* (Frankfurt am Main: Vittorio Klostermann, 1967), p. 143, translation mine.

141. Heidegger, Martin, "Platons Lehre von der Wahrheit," in *Wegmarken*, Vittorio Klostermann (Frankfurt am Main: 1967), p. 143, translation mine.

142. *Ibid.*, p. 130. (. . .*auch die Unverborgenheit noch einen Rang innehält.*)

143. Derrida, op. cit. p. 76.

144. *Ibid.*, p. 86.

145. *Ibid.*, p. 149.

146. *Ibid.*, p. 156.

147. See Chapter 1, p. 20.

148. Derrida, op. cit., p. 158.

149. In Diels, Hermann, *Die Fragmente der Vorsokratiker*, Band I, Weidmannsche Buchverhandlung (Berlin-Grunewald: 1951), fr. 51.

150. Derrida, op. cit., p. 156.

151. Less well-oriented souls are either unable to sustain the vision, rising and sinking as they attempt their ascent, or incapable of the vision of the *eidē* at all, and must "feed on mere opinion." (248a1–b5) They are incapable of discerning opinion as opinion from knowledge in the absence of the vision.

152. "He jerks the bit back even more violently than before, and forces it from between the teeth of the hubristic horse, bloodying its abusive tongue and jaws, forcing its legs and haunches firmly to the ground, and tormenting it with pain." (254e2–4) Tr. Cobb, *Plato's Erotic Dialogues* (Albany: SUNY Press, 1993) p. 111.

153. Like the *Phaedrus*, a myth of recollection accompanies the discussion of virtue in the *Meno*. Also like the *Phaedrus*, the myth at once asserts the possibility of seeing the *eidē* and the need for maintaining strength of soul on this quest.
    In the *Meno*, Socrates refutes Meno's second definition of virtue by *reductio*. Virtue, Meno says, is ruling men. Socrates gives a few counterexamples, such as

children ruling their parents, and slaves ruling at all. But Socrates does not attack the "ruling" part of the definition. Later, he excoriates Meno for his inability to rule himself in thought.

Although it is never declared expressly, it is hinted and never denied that virtue involves *self-rule*. And as Meno is unable to distinguish between what he knows and what he has heard, Socrates' attacks upon him and his insistence that Meno (and Anytus and the slave boy) confront their own ignorance suggest a halting definition of virtue concealed in the folds of the dialogue: virtue is self-rule within the limits of ignorance and knowledge. (See Chapter 4, esp. p. 57–58)

Chapter Ten

154. Its more general meaning is god or goddess, divine power, lot or fortune. In Hesiod, the souls of men in the golden age were called *daimones*, and they formed the link between gods and men.

155. See also *Gorgias*, 489d1, 517b2.

156. This is contrary to the view of A.E. Taylor who, like Hegel, claims that Plato treats "the peculiarity very lightly." ". . .[T]he sign manifested itself sporadically, often on very trivial occasions. . ." Interestingly, Taylor attributes Socrates "shrewd humor" as the antidote to this tendency toward "superstition." [Taylor, A. E., *Socrates* (New York: D. Appleton and Co., 1933), p. 34–38].

In a peculiar way, this worthy insight—which presupposes the very distinction *The Play of the Platonic Dialogues* is at pains to overcome—anticipates the view that playfulness is the most fundamental strain in the dialogues.

157. The Hegelian engagement, however, is on a much more significant plane.

158. Hegel, G.W.F., *Lectures on the History of Philosophy*, vol. 1, tr. Haldane (New York: The Humanities Press, 1963), p. 422. (On occasion, I have altered the translations slightly.)

159. *Ibid.*, p. 422.

160. *Ibid.*, p. 422. (emphasis mine)

161. *Ibid.*, p. 423.

162. *Ibid.*, p. 423.

163. *Ibid.*, p. 424.

164. *Ibid.*, p. 424–5.

165. *Ibid.*, p. 424.

166. Hegel, G.W.F., *Phänomenologie des Geistes* (Hamburg: Felix Meiner Verlag, 1952), p. 12.

167. This is surely the case in Socrates' futile conversation in the *Euthyphro* with the person so named. Euthyphro confounds Socrates' *daimonion* with his own predictions (*proeipon*) of what the gods will do (3b5–c5), and encounters the restraining influence of the Socratic *elenchos*, allied with the *daimonion*, from then on.

168. Nietzsche, in *The Birth of Tragedy*, called this impulse which does not urge forward but restrains, a monstrous defect. "This voice, whenever it comes, always *dissuades*. In this utterly abnormal nature, instinctive wisdom appears only in order to *hinder* conscious knowledge occasionally. While in all productive men it is instinct that is the creative-affirmative force, and consciousness acts critically and dissuasively, in Socrates it is instinct that becomes the critic, and consciousness that becomes the creator—truly a monstrosity *per defectum*." (tr. Kaufmann, Vintage Books (New York: 1967), p. 88.)
    Nietzsche saw a conflict between the "logical" Socrates and the "music-practicing" Socrates, and this distinction is one of the most fruitful in the history of thought about Plato. This interpretation sees the *daimonion* as a function of the play of the dialogues, and its instinctively measure-giving function as entirely in accord with, and indeed part of, the Socratic practice of music.

169. The absence of the *daimonion* when he gave the bad speech indicates the appropriateness of this speech at the time and for the purpose it was given. Socrates' discovery of his friend's inability to discern its badness is the account, from the rational side, of his decision to remain.

170. This issue was raised in the Foreword on p. 6, and will receive fuller treatment in Chapter 12.

171. Sallis, op. cit., p. 532.

172. Cf. Chapter 8, p. 119ff., for a different proposal in the same spirit.

Chapter Eleven

173. See Chapter 8, p. 115.

174. See Chapter 1, p. 19–21.

175. See Chapter 1, p. 17–18.

176. Nor are the works of painters, who suffuse their work with the power of their inspiration as well.

177. See Chapter 3, p. 50ff.

178. "Names cannot be guaranteed by an appeal to their origin nor by an appeal to other names nor by an appeal to that immediate vision befitting a god. The only appeal is an appeal to that which names and *logos* serve to let it be manifest. In the most profound way the *Cratylus* lets the necessity of the appeal become manifest—in the most profound way because it lets this demand stand in all the questionableness

which it has for man. . . ." Sallis, op. cit., p. 310.

179. Cf. Chapter 10, p. 151f.

180. See Chapter 7, passim.

181. While "remedy" (Bloom) or "antidote" (Shorey) aren't incorrect translations, they constrict the play of the text to its detriment.

182. See Chapter 9, p. 125.

183. Cf. p. 78-80.

184. See also p. 18, note 22; and p. 103, note 105.

185. See Chapter 1, p. 20ff.

Chapter Twelve

186. We are ignorant, that is, unless we take them to be the gain of public and/or private powers and comforts. But in that case their connection to justice is not clear at all, since love of gain is excluded from the just soul.

187. The myth with which Socrates ends the *Gorgias* has similar characteristics. Not only are bodies more or less the same after death as they were in life, souls also remain the same. The principal difference is that "all things in the soul are visible (*endēla*)" (524d4–5); that is to say, they are presented in a realm which is at least an analogue of the mortal realm.

188. R. Burger correctly notes that ". . .Socrates' interlacing of words [in 100a3–e4] suggests that the final argument for immortality will be in the service of his demonstration of the eidos of cause, rather that the other way around." (see her *The Phaedo: A Platonic Labyrinth*, Yale University Press (New Haven: 1984), p. 147.

189. See Foreword, p. 6.

190. In the *Charmides*, the charm (*epōdēs*) Socrates learns from the Thracian king Zalmochis will cure a headache or any bodily ache because it first cures the soul, after which the eyes, head and body follow; the charm: beautiful words (*kalous. . .logous*). (see 156a9-157c6)
        As in the *Phaedo*, rigorous *logos* belongs to musical charm in the *Charmides* and introduces measure into both the discourse and to the souls of the ones present, redirecting attention to the (very different) pull of the body in each.

191. By this word, I understand a singer of epodes and one who chants with great charm.

192. See the discussion on *epoden* and *logos* in Chapter 5, p. 78-80.

193. Cf. *Apology* 28b6–29d9.

194. See Chapter 6, p. 83ff.

I. INDEX OF PROPER NAMES

II. INDEX OF DIALOGUES

III. INDEX OF KEY GREEK TERMS

(page listings include plurals and some variants)

IV. INDEX OF TOPICS

Literature and the Sciences of Man

This interdisciplinary series is predicated on the conviction that the inevitable development toward increasing specialization requires as its correlative a movement toward integration between the humanities, social sciences, and natural sciences. Titles in the series will deal with "multidisciplinary" figures, as well as with movements affecting a variety of disciplines. The series editor will also consider manuscripts dealing with methods and strategies in the domains of aesthetic creation, the arts of criticism, and scientific exploration.

Please direct all inquiries to the series editor.

Peter Heller
Dept. of Modern Languages &
    Literatures
SUNY-Buffalo
Buffalo, NY 14260

DATE DUE

JUN 3 0 2004			